LEGAL RESEARCH

IN

CALIFORNIA

LEGAL RESEARCH

IN

CALIFORNIA

FIRST EDITION
1993

JOHN K. HANFT

WATERMELLON BOOKS
SAN FRANCISCO

TABLE OF CONTENTS

ABOUT THIS BOOK   vii

ABOUT THE AUTHOR   vii

DETAILED OUTLINE   ix

CHAPTER 1   THE LEGAL RESEARCH ENVIRONMENT   1

CHAPTER 2   PHYSICAL CHARACTERISTICS OF RESEARCH
                 MATERIALS   21

CHAPTER 3   THE LEGAL PROFESSION   33

CHAPTER 4   THE JUDICIAL BRANCH   43

CHAPTER 5   CASE LAW   67

CHAPTER 6   THE LEGISLATIVE BRANCH   97

CHAPTER 7   CONSTITUTIONAL AND STATUTORY LAW   113

CHAPTER 8   ADMINISTRATIVE LAW   131

CHAPTER 9   COMMENTARY AND ANALYSIS   153

CHAPTER 10   PRACTICE WORKS AND FORM BOOKS   173

CHAPTER 11   VERIFYING AND UPDATING INFORMATION   195

CHAPTER 12   COMPUTERIZED RESEARCH   203

CHAPTER 13   RESOURCES IN MAJOR PRACTICE AREAS   221

INDEX   245

ABOUT THIS BOOK

This book is a basic legal research guide with two intended functions: (1) As a textbook, it is designed to introduce students to the fundamental concepts and standard publications used in California legal research. (2) As a reference book, it is designed to provide practitioners with quick answers to common questions about legal research and law practice in California. Generally, the focus is on California materials, although some national and federal sources are included.

The text is divided into chapters, each covering a broad research topic. Chapters are subdivided into sections, which are linked by cross-references to related material in other sections. An alphabetical index of key words and topics provides section references. Both the index and the chapter outlines may be used to locate relevant material.

Like the law itself, legal research is a fluid discipline. Publishers come and go, publications expand and contract, features and format vary with the seasons. Thus, the reader should view the material presented in this book, especially sections describing the features of various publications, as illustrative, not definitive, information.

Comments, suggestions, and questions about this book should be addressed to the publisher: Watermelon Books, 2424 30th Avenue, San Francisco, California 94116-2210.

John K. Hanft
San Francisco

ABOUT THE AUTHOR

John K. Hanft has been a member of the State Bar of California and an editor at a California law book publishing company since 1976. He also teaches legal research and lectures at seminars for lawyers, paralegals, and law students on various legal research and writing topics.

DETAILED OUTLINE

CHAPTER 1

THE LEGAL RESEARCH ENVIRONMENT

§1.1	Sources of Law	2
§1.2	Primary and Secondary Authority	2
§1.3	Mandatory and Persuasive Authority	3
§1.4	Standard Legal Classifications	4
§1.5	Major Law Book Publishers	6
§1.6	Publishers' Catalogs	9
§1.7	Legal Service Providers	10
§1.8	Libraries	10
§1.9	Library Classification Systems	11
§1.10	Pathfinders	12
§1.11	Bibliographic Sources	12
§1.12	Legal Research Guides	13
§1.13	Dictionaries	15
§1.14	Abbreviations	15
§1.15	Citation	16
§1.16	Legal Terminology	17
§1.17	Research Tips and Strategy	18

CHAPTER 2

PHYSICAL CHARACTERISTICS OF RESEARCH MATERIALS

§2.1	Format	22
§2.2	Section	22
§2.3	Outline	23
§2.4	Tables	23
§2.5	Index	24
§2.6	Cross Reference	24
§2.7	Collateral Reference	25
§2.8	Annotation	25
§2.9	Binding	25
§2.10	Single Volumes and Sets	26
§2.11	Supplementation	26
§2.12	Annual Replacement Volumes	27
§2.13	Looseleaf Format	28
§2.14	Selectively Revised Volumes	28
§2.15	New Editions and Series	29
§2.16	Advance Sheets	30
§2.17	Cumulations	30

§2.18   Shelving and Filing Instructions   31
§2.19   Microfiche   31

CHAPTER 3

THE LEGAL PROFESSION

§3.1   Regulation of Law Practice   34
§3.2   State Bar of California   34
§3.3   State Bar Rules   35
§3.4   Local and Specialty Associations   36
§3.5   National Associations   37
§3.6   State Bar and ABA Sections   37
§3.7   Lawyer Directories   39
§3.8   Legal Ethics   40
§3.9   Continuing Legal Education   41
§3.10   Law Schools   41

CHAPTER 4

THE JUDICIAL BRANCH

§4.1   In General   44
§4.2   Jurisdiction   44
§4.3   Trial and Appellate Courts   46
§4.4   Court Records and Fees   47
§4.5   Federal Judicial System   48
§4.6   California Judicial System   50
§4.7   Supreme Court   51
§4.8   Courts of Appeal   52
§4.9   Superior Courts   53
§4.10   Municipal and Justice Courts   54
§4.11   Judicial Council   54
§4.12   Reporter of Decisions   55
§4.13   Law Revision Commission   56
§4.14   Commission on Judicial Appointments   56
§4.15   Commission on Judicial Performance   57
§4.16   California Judges Association   57
§4.17   Center for Judicial Education and Research 57
§4.18   Judicial Council Forms   58
§4.19   California Rules of Court   59
§4.20   Local Court Rules and Forms   61
§4.21   Federal Court Rules and Forms   61
§4.22   Published Rules   62
§4.23   Jury Instructions   64
§4.24   Court and Judges Directories   65

CHAPTER 5

CASE LAW

§5.1	Common Law	68
§5.2	Court Opinions	69
§5.3	Reports and Reporters	69
§5.4	Publication of Opinions in California	71
§5.5	Advance Reports	72
§5.6	Bancroft Whitney Advance Sheets	74
§5.7	West Advance Sheets	76
§5.8	Appellate Department	77
§5.9	Selective Publication	78
§5.10	Depublication	79
§5.11	Time Deadlines in the Appellate Process	80
§5.12	Subsequent History Table	80
§5.13	California Citation Guide	81
§5.14	Federal Cases	82
§5.15	West Reporter System	84
§5.16	Tips for Finding Cases	85
§5.17	Case Briefs	86
§5.18	Digests	87
§5.19	Bancroft Whitney Digests	88
§5.20	West Digests	89
§5.21	West Key Number System	90
§5.22	ALR (American Law Reports)	91
§5.23	Restatements	93

CHAPTER 6

THE LEGISLATIVE BRANCH

§6.1	In General	98
§6.2	Federal Legislative System	98
§6.3	California Legislative System	98
§6.4	The Lifecycle of Legislation	99
§6.5	California Assembly Standing Committees	100
§6.6	California Senate Standing Committees	101
§6.7	Statutory Numbering	102
§6.8	Bill Numbering	102
§6.9	Enactment Numbering	103
§6.10	Federal Session Laws	103
§6.11	California Session Laws	104
§6.12	Advance Legislative Services	105
§6.13	Legislative History	106
§6.14	Legislative History Services	107
§6.15	California Legislative Sources	107

§6.16   Federal Legislative Sources   108
§6.17   CCH Congressional Index   109
§6.18   U.S. Code Congressional and   110
        Administrative News (USCCAN)
§6.19   Congressional Information Service (CIS)   111
§6.20   Pending Legislation   112

CHAPTER 7

CONSTITUTIONAL AND STATUTORY LAW

§7.1   Constitutional Law   114
§7.2   California Constitution   114
§7.3   Codification   115
§7.4   United States Code   116
§7.5   California Codes   117
§7.6   Annotated Codes   118
§7.7   Unannotated Codes   120
§7.8   Statutes in Electronic Form   121
§7.9   Statutory Indexes   122
§7.10   Code Numbering   123
§7.11   Prior Law and Former Section   125
§7.12   Effective Date of California Legislation   125
§7.13   Popular Name Tables   126
§7.14   Tips for Finding Statutes   126
§7.15   Numbering of Propositions   127
§7.16   Uniform Laws   128
§7.17   Uniform Acts Adopted in California   129

CHAPTER 8

ADMINISTRATIVE LAW

§8.1   In General   132
§8.2   Guides and Directories   132
§8.3   California Executive Branch   133
§8.4   Administrative Agencies   138
§8.5   Secretary of State   142
§8.6   Department of Justice   142
§8.7   Attorney General Opinions   143
§8.8   Franchise Tax Board   144
§8.9   State Board of Equalization   144
§8.10   Department of Corporations   144
§8.11   Public Utilities Commission   145
§8.12   Opinions and Services   145
§8.13   California Code of Regulations   146

§8.14   Code of Federal Regulations   148
§8.15   Finding and Updating Federal Regulations   149
§8.16   Looseleaf Services   150
§8.17   Tips for Finding Administrative Law   151

CHAPTER 9

COMMENTARY AND ANALYSIS

§9.1   Treatises   154
§9.2   Witkin   155
§9.3   Encyclopedias   156
§9.4   Law School Texts   157
§9.5   Legal Periodicals   158
§9.6   Classification of Law Reviews   158
§9.7   Use of Law Reviews   160
§9.8   Law Reviews in California   161
§9.9   Periodical Indexes   163
§9.10   Newsletters   165
§9.11   Newsletters in California   165
§9.12   Newspapers   168
§9.13   Sources of Comparative Law   169
§9.14   Deskbooks   170

CHAPTER 10

PRACTICE WORKS AND FORM BOOKS

§10.1   In General   174
§10.2   Bancroft Whitney   174
§10.3   CEB   175
§10.4   CEB Action Guides   176
§10.5   CEB Practice Books   177
§10.6   Matthew Bender   184
§10.7   Parker   186
§10.8   Rutter Group   188
§10.9   Other California Practice Works   189
§10.10   CLE Program Materials   192
§10.11   Self-Help Books   192

CHAPTER 11

VERIFYING AND UPDATING INFORMATION

§11.1   Finding Current Information   196

§11.2	Verifying Legal Authorities	197
§11.3	Shepard's Citations	198
§11.4	California Authorities in Shepard's	200
§11.5	National Authorities in Shepard's	202

CHAPTER 12

COMPUTERIZED RESEARCH

§12.1	In General	204
§12.2	Software	205
§12.3	Online Databases	207
§12.4	Dialog	209
§12.5	Lexis	210
§12.6	Westlaw	213
§12.7	Periodicals and Periodical Indexes	216
§12.8	CD-ROM	217
§12.9	California CD-ROM Products	217
§12.10	National CD-ROM Products	219

CHAPTER 13

RESOURCES IN MAJOR PRACTICE AREAS

§13.1	Administrative Law	222
§13.2	Business and Corporate Law	222
§13.3	Civil Litigation and Evidence	224
§13.4	Contracts and Commercial Law	227
§13.5	Criminal Law and Procedure	227
§13.6	Environmental Law, Energy, and Water	229
§13.7	Estate Planning, Trusts, and Probate	231
§13.8	Family and Juvenile Law	232
§13.9	Federal Practice	233
§13.10	Financial Institutions and Insurance	234
§13.11	Intellectual Property	235
§13.12	International Law	235
§13.13	Labor, Employment and Workers' Compensation	236
§13.14	Law Practice and Legal Services	238
§13.15	Real and Personal Property; Landlord-Tenant	239
§13.16	Taxation	241
§13.17	Torts and Products Liability	242

CHAPTER 1

THE LEGAL RESEARCH ENVIRONMENT

This chapter introduces fundamental concepts involved in legal research and provides general information about research sources.

§1.1	Sources of Law	2
§1.2	Primary and Secondary Authority	2
§1.3	Mandatory and Persuasive Authority	3
§1.4	Standard Legal Classifications	4
§1.5	Major Law Book Publishers	6
§1.6	Publishers' Catalogs	9
§1.7	Legal Service Providers	10
§1.8	Libraries	10
§1.9	Library Classification Systems	11
§1.10	Pathfinders	12
§1.11	Bibliographic Sources	12
§1.12	Legal Research Guides	13
§1.13	Dictionaries	15
§1.14	Abbreviations	15
§1.15	Citation	16
§1.16	Legal Terminology	17
§1.17	Research Tips and Strategy	18

———————————

§1.1   SOURCES OF LAW

Broadly speaking, law is the set of rules created by society to regulate the activities of people and the business of government. Legal research is the process of discovering and articulating those rules. This process is complex for many reasons, including the following:

(1) Law comes from many branches and levels of government: federal, state, and local; legislative, executive, and judicial. In addition to the federal government and its many agencies, the fifty states, and thousands of cities, counties, and special districts create law. The people, through initiative measures or conventions, produce constitutional law, legislatures produce statutory law, executive departments and agencies produce administrative law, and courts produce case law.

(2) Various government entities generate law in ways that serve the needs of government, rather than legal researchers. For example, the chronological publication of court opinions preserves a public record of judicial business but is not much help to a researcher looking for cases about the same subject matter.

(3) Publishers of legal research materials tend to respect governmental distinctions between civil and criminal law; state and federal law; substantive and procedural law. (On these distinctions, see §1.4.) This means that all the law a researcher needs to know is rarely, if ever, discoverable in one location.

§1.2   PRIMARY AND SECONDARY AUTHORITY

It is convenient to categorize legal research materials according to content, as follows:

(1) _Primary Authority_. Primary authority refers to the words of the law itself, as articulated by the various branches of government. Broadly defined, the term includes constitutions and charters, statutes and ordinances, legislative documents, court opinions and rules, and administrative decisions and regulations.

(2) <u>Secondary Authority</u>. Secondary authority refers to editorial comment or discussion, as articulated by individuals, legal entities, and commercial publishers. The term includes encyclopedias, treatises, legal periodicals and law reviews, looseleaf services, annotations, uniform laws, and restatements.

(3) <u>Finding Tools</u>. Finding tools are those volumes or features of legal publications that help identify primary or secondary authority. The term includes digests, citators, indexes, and tables.

These distinctions, of course, are inexact. Looseleaf services and annotated codes typically include both primary and secondary authority, and nearly all law books include finding tools of some kind.

§1.3   MANDATORY AND PERSUASIVE AUTHORITY

Not all legal authority is of equal weight. Authority that must be followed is called mandatory authority. Authority that may, but need not, be followed is called persuasive authority. In addition, some mandatory authority is more mandatory than other. That is, a higher authority takes priority over a lower authority. Generally, the hierarchy of mandatory authority in California is as follows:

(1) United States Constitution
(2) Federal statutes
(3) California Constitution
(4) California statutes
(5) California and federal cases from higher courts on point
(6) California Code of Regulations
(7) California court rules
(8) Local ordinances

"On point" refers to statements of law that are necessary to the decision. Frequently, cases make statements of law that are not necessary to resolve the dispute at issue. These statements are not mandatory and are known as dicta or dictum (from obiter dictum = collateral word). For example, a case involving sex discrimination may make statements of law involving both sex discrimination and age discrimination. The statements concerning age discrimination are dicta and persuasive only.

Persuasive authority consists of all authority that is not mandatory, including the following:

(1) An opinion of a parallel or lower California court
(2) A federal court opinion on California law
(3) An opinion from another state
(4) Law Revision Commission Comments
(5) Regulatory decisions
(6) Attorney General opinions
(7) Jury instructions
(8) Restatements
(9) Treatises, law review articles, other secondary sources

§1.4 STANDARD LEGAL CLASSIFICATIONS

Over time, established ways of classifying and arranging the law have developed. These standard concepts provide useful shorthand for practitioners. They are especially important for researchers because law books tend to reflect the way the standard classifications present the law.

(1) _Substance and Procedure_. Substantive law refers generally to the legal principles that define and govern rights, responsibilities and liabilities. The substantive law of real property, for example, includes the rules that express a landowner's legal duty to guests, business invitees, and trespassers. Procedural law refers generally to the legal principles that govern the enforcement of rights and responsibilities in court. The procedural law of real property, for example, include the principles governing pleadings, discovery, right to a jury trial, and so forth in a business invitee's action to enforce a landowner's liability for injury.

(2) _Civil and Criminal_. Criminal law involves a public wrong and refers to an action by the state to enforce the statutes that define crimes. If the defendant faces the possibility of being

jailed or imprisoned, the matter is criminal. Civil law involves a private wrong and refers to an action between private parties or involving the government in which no crime has been committed. The distinction become somewhat blurry, for example, in civil actions by the government and in quasi-criminal proceedings (like involuntary commitment).

(3) <u>Matters of State Law or Federal Law</u>. Many areas of law have both a state and a federal component, and a single transaction may have local law, state law, and federal law consequences (e.g., taxation). However, there are areas of law which tend to be matters of exclusively federal or exclusively state concern. Some common examples are:

(a) <u>Matters of Federal Law</u>. Admiralty; bankruptcy; patent, copyright, trademark; native Americans; federal funds and programs.

(b) <u>Matters of State Law</u>. Real property; decedent's estates; personal injury; contacts; regulation of professions and businesses.

(c) <u>Matters of Both State and Federal Law</u>. Taxation; environmental protection; health and welfare; transportation; securities; financial institutions; crimes.

(4) <u>Transactions and Litigation</u>. This distinction, mostly observed by law book publishers, is a very rough line between what lawyers do in the office with respect to transactions involving clients and what lawyers do in court or to prepare for litigation. For example, a form for a real property lease will be in a volume of "legal" or "transactional" forms, while a complaint for breach of the terms of a real property lease will be in a volume of "pleading" or "practice" forms.

(5) <u>Law and Equity</u>. The distinction between law and equity refers to the distinction in English common law between law courts and equity courts. For historical reasons, law courts were generally authorized to provide only "legal" relief, in the form of money damages. In response, equity courts gradually developed with authority to fashion more flexible (and just) remedies, such as recision of a contract or injunctive relief (an order to do or not

do specified acts).   In the United States, this distinction between courts is rarely observed; any court may provide both legal and equitable relief. Some vestiges of the distinction remain, however, in determining those situations in which the right to a jury trial is available, because a jury trial was not available in equity courts.

§1.5   MAJOR LAW BOOK PUBLISHERS

     The focus in legal research materials tends to be on publishers, rather than authors, partly because the field is dominated by a handful of large publishers and partly because many research materials are produced by multiple authors, an editorial staff, or an executive or legislative agency, and thus lack an identifiable author.
     Basic information about law book publishers and information providers may be found in many sources. Law Books and Serials in Print (see §1.11) includes a list of law publishers and vendors. The following publishers and vendors are significant in the California legal market:

Bancroft Whitney
P.O. Box 7005
San Francisco, CA 94120-7005
(800) 848-4000

Barclays Law Publishers
400 Oyster Point Drive, #500
South San Francisco, CA 94080
(415) 800-3600

California Journal Press
1714 Capitol Avenue
Sacramento, CA 95814
(916) 444-2840

CEB (Continuing Education of the Bar)
2300 Shattuck Avenue
Berkeley, CA 94704
(510) 642-8000; (800) 924-3924

CCH (Commerce Clearing House)
4025 West Peterson Avenue
Chicago, IL 60646
(800) 248-3248; (312) 583-8500

CIS (Congressional Information Service)
4520 East-West Highway, Suite 800
Bethesda, MD 20814
(800) 638-8380

Daily Journal
P.O. Box 54026
Los Angeles, CA 90054-0026
(213) 625-2141
1390 Market Street, Suite 910
San Francisco, CA 94120
(415) 558-9888

H.W.Wilson
950 University Avenue
Bronx, NY 10452
(800) 367-6770

Information Access
362 Lakeside Drive
Foster City, CA 94404
(415) 378-5000; (800) 227-8431

LCP (Lawyers Cooperative Publishing)
Aqueduct Building
Rochester, NY 19694
(800) 527-0430

Martindale Hubbell
121 Chalon Road
New Providence, NJ 07974
(800) 521-8110

Matthew Bender
2101 Webster Street
Oakland, CA 94612
(415) 446-7100: (800) 833-9844; (800) 223-1940 (CD-ROM)

Mead Data Central (Lexis)
P.O. Box 933
Dayton, OH 45401
(800) 543-6862, (513) 865-6800

Nolo Press
950 Parker Street
Berkeley, CA 94710
(510) 548-5902

Parker Publications
P.O. Box 9040
Carlsbad, CA 92018-9040
(800) 452-9873

Prentice Hall
15 Columbus Circle
New York, NY 10452
(800) 922-0579; (800) 223-0231

Recorder
625 Polk Street
San Francisco, CA 94102
(415) 749-5406

R.R. Bowker
121 Chanlon Road
New Providence, NJ 07974
(800) 521-8110; (800) 323-3288 (electronic publishing)

Rutter Group
15760 Ventura Blvd, Suite 630
Encino, CA 91436
(818) 990-3260; (800) 747-3161

Shepard's / McGraw Hill
P.O. Box 35300
Colorado Springs, CO 80935-3530
(800) 541-3334; (800) 525-2474

West Publishing Company
50 West Kellog Blvd
St. Paul, MN 55164-0526
(800) 325-8660, (800) 688-6363 (reference attorneys)
(800) 328-9352; (800) 937-8529 (Westlaw; CD-ROM)

§1.6   PUBLISHERS' CATALOGS

Most legal publishers produce catalogs, brochures, or demonstration disks explaining or touting their products. If up-to-date, these materials can be useful for quickly identifying relevant publications and finding the right tools to investigate an unfamiliar area of law.

Many publishers and vendors have customer service numbers to answer the questions of subscribers. These often appear on the first page of a volume's supplement. Providers of electronic products frequently offer individual or group training to subscribers, which may qualify for MCLE credit (see §3.2). Some publishers also provide free or low-cost instructional materials to instructors or subscribers. The most common include:

(1) Bancroft Whitney: Deering's Chart of the Courts; How to Use ALR 5th

(2) West: Law Finder; Sample Pages; How to Use West's California Digest, 2d

(3) CCH: Finding the answers to federal tax questions; The Standard Federal Tax Reporter [filmstrip]

(4) Shepard's: Questions and Answers About Shepard's Citations; How to Shepardize [video]

§1.7   LEGAL SERVICE PROVIDERS

There are hundreds of providers of services for lawyers, including computer software systems, information brokers, research, personnel, document searching and filing, deposition summaries, private investigators, litigation support, jury and expert witness services, courtroom graphics and exhibits, and so forth. Providers advertise and many newspapers and periodicals provide periodic lists. (On legislative history services, see §6.14.) Some illustrative examples include the following:

(1)   Washington Service Bureau; SEC document retrieval, research, and filing; 655 15th Street NW, Washington, DC 20005, (800) 289-1057

(2)   Duns Legal Search; searches for public record filings nationwide, e.g., UCC filings, business registrations, bankruptcies; (908) 665-5446

(3)   Boalt Express; Boalt Hall Library, U.C. Berkeley; document delivery service; (800) 832-4586

(4)   County Law Retrieval Service; Los Angeles County Law Library; document delivery service; (213) 957-5033

(5)   Document Delivery Services, Columbia Law School Library; (800) 332-4529

§1.8   LIBRARIES

Each county has a county law library for the use of the bench, the bar and the public, and most law school libraries are open to lawyers. Those which are government depository libraries must provide public access to their government documents. Main public libraries are often the best source for newspapers and government documents. Some county law libraries allow selected volumes to be checked out. In San Francisco, for example, local judges, government officers, and lawyers may borrow materials for short period of time, subject to the librarian's discretion for books of special character or in frequent use.

§1.9   LIBRARY CLASSIFICATION SYSTEMS

Library of Congress System. The call number of an item in the Library of Congress system consists of two parts, letters and numbers. Letters denote broad classifications of subject matter and large geographical areas. K is the classification for Law. KF refers to law of the United States, and other two letter classifications refer to other geographical areas of the world (e.g., KH = South America; KP = Asia). A three letter classification indicates a part or parts of the geographical area represented by the two letter classification. Frequently, the third letter indicates states or provinces beginning with the third letter (e.g. KFC = California; Colorado; Connecticut). KFX = the law of individual U.S. cities. Numbers denote smaller topical subdivisions of the main subject matter. In the KF classification, there are over 250 of these classifications (e.g., 165 = Uniform State Laws; 726-745 = trusts and trustees; 2076-2140 = public utilities; 9601-9760 = criminal procedure). For detailed information, see Library of Congress Classification Schedules (multivolume); Gale.

Dewey Decimal System. The call number of an item in the Dewey decimal system consists of a decimal element and an alphabetical element. Whole numbers from 000 to 999 are divided into ten broad categories, which are divided into smaller topical areas, with decimals added for additional subcategories. Within each decimal classification, books are generally arranged alphabetically by the author's last name or (in the absence of an author) by the main subject entry for the work. The classification for law, 340, is arranged as follows:

    341   International law
    342   Constitutional and administrative law
    343   Miscellaneous public law
    344   Social law
    345   Criminal law
    346   Private law

347   Civil procedure
348   Statutes, regulations, cases

§1.10   PATHFINDERS

A pathfinder is a collection of basic information on a research question, practice, or publication. Pathfinders generally explain how to do something, describe a publication and its use, or list sources for information about a topic. "How to Compile a Legislative History" is an example. Pathfinders were originally developed as a teaching tool in library school, but are now becoming available in firms and libraries. Creating a personal pathfinder can be a useful way for legal research students to master unfamiliar publications and sources. (For discussion of pathfinders, see Trotta, A Map Through the Maze, California Lawyer, February 1991, page 53.) The topical material in Chapter 13 reflects some elements common to pathfinders. A topical pathfinder might identify relevant material in the following areas:

(1) State and federal statutes
(2) Significant cases
(3) Bibliographies
(4) Specialized journals, newsletters, and looseleafs
(5) Journal articles
(6) Treatises
(7) Encyclopedia and digest chapters
(8) West key numbers
(9) ALR annotations
(10) Databases, compact discs, online services
(11) Organizations, experts, and regulatory agencies

§1.11   BIBLIOGRAPHIC SOURCES

Many bibliographic sources about law books and legal information are available, including some of the deskbooks listed in §9.14. The following are illustrative:

The Bibliographic Guide to Law; G.K. Hall & Co.; hardcover; two volumes; annual edition. The publication is an alphabetical, subject matter index to publications cataloged by the Library of Congress in the previous year in the areas of law, criminology, forensic medicine, international relations, etc. It provides Library of Congress cataloging information.

Law Books and Serials in Print - A Multimedia Sourcebook; R.R. Bowker; hardcover; 3 volumes; annual edition; updated with cumulative softcover quarterly issues; indexed by subject, title, and author. This publication is an annotated bibliography of print and non-print legal material, including books, serials, cassettes, software, online databases, microforms, and publishers.

Encyclopedia of Legal Information Sources (2nd edition); Gale; hardcover; one volume; arranged alphabetically by subject.

Law Books in Print (6th edition); Glanville Publishers; 6 volumes.

International Legal Books in Print; 1990; R.R. Bowker; hardcover; two volumes.

The Lawyer's Almanac; annual; Prentice Hall; information about lawyers, law schools, courts, and government; statutory summaries; commonly used abbreviations.

Legal Information Alert; newsletter about legal publications, databases, and research techniques; ten issues a year; Alert Publications.

§1.12   LEGAL RESEARCH GUIDES

There are numerous legal research texts and guides, among them:

California Law Guide (2d edition) by Henke; 1976; Parker; hardcover; pamphlet supplement.

Fundamentals of Legal Research (5th edition) by Jacobstein and Mersky; 1990; Foundation Press. The abridged version is called Legal Research Illustrated.

How to Find the Law (9th edition) by Cohen, Berring and Olsen; 1989; West. The abridged version is called Finding the Law.

Find the Law in the Library: A Guide to Legal Research; 1989; American Library Association.

Legal Research in a Nutshell (4th edition) by Cohen; 1985; West.

Legal Research Manual (2d edition) by Wren and Wren; 1988; Adams and Ambrose Publishing.

Computer-Assisted Legal Research by Griffith; 1991; Anderson Publishing Company; softcover; one volume.

Using Computers in Legal Research: A Guide to LEXIS and WESTLAW; Adams and Ambrose Publishing.

Specialized Legal Research; 1987; Little Brown.

Practical Approaches to Legal Research by Olsen and Berring; 1988; Hayworth Press.

The Process of Legal Research: Successful Strategies (2d edition) by Kunz et al; 1989; Little Brown.

Guide to International Legal Research; 1990; Butterworth Legal Publishers; softcover; one volume.

Legal Research, Writing, and Advocacy by Gilmer; 1987; Anderson Publishing Company; softcover; one volume.

§1.13   DICTIONARIES

A number of general and specialized legal dictionaries are available, including the following:

Ballantine's Law Dictionary (3d edition); 1969; LCP; hardcover; one volume.

Black's Law Dictionary (6th edition); 1991; West; hardcover; one volume; electronic version available.

A Dictionary of Modern Legal Usage; 1987; Oxford University Press.

West's Legal Thesaurus/Dictionary; 1986; West; hardcover; one volume.

West's Tax Law Dictionary; 1992; West; softcover; one volume.

West's Spanish/English English/Spanish Law Dictionary; 1992; West; softcover; one volume.

Butterworth's Spanish/English Legal Dictionary; 1991; Butterworth Legal Publishers; hardcover; two volumes.

§1.14   ABBREVIATIONS

Comprehending legal citation requires familiarity with standard legal abbreviations. Many legal dictionaries and legal research guides include standard abbreviations either as a table or within the alphabetical listings. For example, The Lawyer's Almanac (see §1.11) includes a table of commonly used abbreviations. Standard abbreviations are also used in Harvard Law Review's Uniform System of Citation (see §1.15). Nearly all law books contain a table of abbreviations used in that volume. (See Bieber's Dictionary of Legal Abbreviation; W.S. Hein; 1988; one volume.)

§1.15   CITATION

In the law, "citation" refers to an abbreviated, shorthand way to refer to or "cite" a legal authority or reference. The idea is to quickly tell just enough information to allow the reader to find the authority. Proper citation depends largely on context; what is appropriate (or required) for citing authorities in appellate briefs may not be appropriate in law review articles or internal memoranda. Although universal citation rules do not exist, some conventions are generally observed. The citations used throughout this book illustrate conventional format. There are a number of ways to determine what the citation of an authority should be:

(1)   The authority itself (usually on the back of the title page) may illustrate how it is to be cited.

(2)   The California Style Manual (3d edition) (1986) provides style rules for opinions in California courts. Sold by the California Department of General Services, P.O. Box 1015, North Highlands, CA 95660.

(3)   The Bluebook: A Uniform System of Citation (15th) (the Harvard Bluebook) provides detailed rules of citation appropriate for law review articles. Published by the Harvard Law Review Association. These guidelines are widely followed.

(4)   The University of Chicago Manual of Legal Citation (the Chicago Maroon Book) is a concise alternative to the Harvard Bluebook.

For purposes of citation, there are two kind of law books:

(1)   Books intended as a permanent record of legal business, which, in theory at least, are intended to remain on the library shelf until the end of recorded time. Case reporters, session laws, law reviews, and ALR annotations are examples. As a general rule, books in this category are cited by page number.

(2) Books intended to have a finite useful life, which, at some future time, are likely to be replaced or superseded. Digests, encyclopedias, treatises, and practice works are examples. As a general rule, books in this category are cited by section number.

§1.16   LEGAL TERMINOLOGY

For a variety of reasons, not the least of which is reliance on the common law (see §5.1), the law is overburdened with jargon. Frequently the law uses archaic terminology or multiple terms to describe identical subject matter. For example, who but a trained researcher would expect to find employment cases under a heading "master and servant" or know that divorce could be covered under the topics "husband and wife," "domestic relations," "family law" and "dissolution"? The uninitiated often thrash about because they either do not know the meaning of legal terms of art (e.g., tort) or impose non-legal meanings where particular legal meanings are intended (e.g., judgment).

There is no quick fix for the jargon problem. For those unfamiliar with legal terminology, extra time studying indexes (see §2.5), dictionaries (see §1.13), and background material is time well spent. Three additional sources give a quick picture of the scope of an area of law:

(1) Encyclopedias. An alphabetical list of chapter titles is often included in each volume. (On encyclopedias, see §9.3.)

(2) Digests. An alphabetical list or topical arrangement of digest topics is often included in each volume. (On digests, see §5.18.)

(3) Deering's. The General Index to Deering's California Codes Annotated contains a subject mattery summary of topics covered in the California statutes. (On Deering's, see §7.6.)

§1.17   RESEARCH TIPS AND STRATEGY

Later sections include specific tips for finding cases (see §5.16), statutes (see §7.14), and administrative law (see §8.17). The following research rules are of general application:

(1)   Keep an accurate record of sources examined, including date, name of publication, volume, chapter, section number, and scope of coverage

(2)   For each statement of law, record the legal authority and the source of the information, and preserve the distinction between the authority and the source

(3)   Keep research up to date by checking supplements, advance sheets, advance services, new material, citators, and newspapers

(4)   Check competing publications for additional information and to verify that coverage is complete

(5)   Ask experts, including practitioners, librarians, government agencies, publishers, and special interest groups; use the telephone

(6)   Become familiar with publishers and vendors and their products and customer services, including 800 numbers; examine each new publication to understand its content, features, scope, and limitations

The following techniques may be helpful in analyzing and solving legal problems:

(1)   Understand the context of the problem. What are the client's objective, status, characteristics, and limitations?

(2)   Examine the problem in terms of broad legal classifications (see §1.4). Is the problem state or federal, substantive or procedural, civil or criminal?

(3) Prepare a list of search terms, both legal and factual, that highlights the various aspects of the problem. (On legal terminology, see §1.16; on indexes, see §2.5.)

(4) Look for legislative, judicial, and administrative components of primary law. Looks for commentary, analysis, and practice advice.

(5) Examine the standard research sources in the practice areas that relate to the problem. (On resources in major practice areas, see §13.1 et seq.)

(6) As a general rule, for California problems, begin with the annotated codes (see §7.6), Witkin (see §9.2), CEB practice books (see §10.5), and ALR (see §5.22).

CHAPTER 2

PHYSICAL CHARACTERISTICS OF RESEARCH MATERIALS

This chapter examines the physical characteristics of legal materials and identifies basic conventions used in legal publishing.

§2.1	Format	22
§2.2	Section	22
§2.3	Outline	23
§2.4	Tables	23
§2.5	Index	24
§2.6	Cross Reference	24
§2.7	Collateral Reference	25
§2.8	Annotation	25
§2.9	Binding	25
§2.10	Single Volumes and Sets	26
§2.11	Supplementation	26
§2.12	Annual Replacement Volumes	27
§2.13	Looseleaf Format	28
§2.14	Selectively Revised Volumes	28
§2.15	New Editions and Series	29
§2.16	Advance Sheets	30
§2.17	Cumulations	30
§2.18	Shelving and Filing Instructions	31
§2.19	Microfiche	31

_____

§2.1   FORMAT

While legal materials have been published traditionally as hardcover books, many sources are also or alternatively available in other formats, including softcover books, looseleafs and pamphlet binders, pamphlets, newspapers, documents, microfiche, floppy disks, compact discs, and online databases. In addition, most legal information is provided, in one form or another, by competing vendors or publishers. For example, many public records are available from government agencies in one format and from commercial publishers in another. Thus, careful researchers check the competition for a complete picture or when an answer is illusive.

The term "slip" refers to the original format of public material, generally court opinions. Thus, printed opinions provided by courts are "slip opinions," and laws when first enacted are "slip laws." Courts with computer bulletin boards provide slip opinions in print and electronic form.

§2.2   SECTION

The basic unit of text in many lawbooks is the section, which is designated by the section symbol (§). For example, statutes, treatises, encyclopedias, form books, and practice works are generally divided into sections. A section consists of a block of text about a single topic, which is identified by the section number and often by a heading or title as well. Sections vary in length from a few lines to several pages.

Sections are numbered consecutively, either throughout the publication or within chapters. Except where statutes are numbered by the legislature (as in California), section numbers are generally provided by the author or publisher. Frequently, decimals are used to identify the chapter as well as the section. Thus, §6.37 refers to the thirty-seventh section of chapter 6. Note that numbering systems sometimes use a term other than "section" but have many of the same characteristics of sections: e.g., (1) West Publishing Company uses a system of classification known as the key number system (see §5.21); (2) CCH looseleaf services used paragraph numbers.

Material that is divided into sections is generally referred to or cited by section, rather than by page number. This practice provides more reliable access to supplements and replacement volumes than the citation of page numbers.

§2.3   OUTLINE

The outline or scheme functions as a table of contents but is generally far more detailed than a traditional (non-legal) table of contents. Usually, text is divided into divisions, parts, chapters, articles, and sections, in what is intended to be an ordered, topical arrangement. The outline reveals the structure at a glance and allows a knowledgeable user to find information on point more quickly than by using a conventional index. A condensed outline shows the divisions, parts, chapters, and articles, but not individual sections. A detailed or complete outline includes individual section numbers and headings as well.

§2.4   TABLES

Because the law relies on authorities that are frequently discussed and cited in legal reference books, it is often easier to find the relevant section of text by pinpointing the location in the text where the authority is discussed or cited than to locate relevant material using a conventional index. Thus, many reference books include tables listing the cases, statutes, rules, or other authorities cited in the text. Tables of statutes, rules and other items with an identifiable number are arranged in numerical order. Tables of cases are alphabetically arranged by the names of the parties, either plaintiffs only or both plaintiffs and defendants. Popular name tables identify legal authorities, especially statutes, by common or popular names. Parallel reference tables link material in a replaced volume with material in its successor.

§2.5 INDEX

While the best indexes use natural language, legal indexes are generally arranged by words or phrases that describe factual situations or legal concepts. (On legal terminology, see §1.16.)

Indexes frequently include two or more levels of entry, to reflect the usual arrangement of legal material in broad categories (e.g., family law) and narrower subcategories (e.g., marriage). Where the same information may be identified by two or three common legal terms, Indexes include or should include cross references. Thus, entries for "divorce," dissolution," and "domestic relations" may all cross-refer to "family law." Often cross references are mechanically produced, sometimes with unfortunate results. Thus, an entry under "Logs and Timber" may refer to "Boards and Commissions."

Many law books are part of a multivolume set. It is common in this situation for each chapter or volume or group of volumes to have an index and for the entire set to have an index (called a "general" index). The annotated California codes, for example, have a separate index for each of the codes and a general index for all the codes. Usually, the indexes to particular chapters or volumes are more detailed and more timely than the general index.

When an area is unfamiliar, a researcher should make a short list of key words related to the topic, derived from the facts or existing knowledge. In addition to things, places, people, acts or omissions, and legal issues and actions, the list should include broader and narrower categories, synonyms and antonyms, related procedural terms, and the names of relevant agencies. This provides a core of possible index entries (or computerized search terms) that should account for all relevant material.

§2.6 CROSS REFERENCE

Generally, a cross reference refers to another portion of the same index, chapter, or set of books in which the reference occurs. Publishers provide cross references to help users make connections between related material. For example, following the statute defining burglary, a cross reference might point out the location of the statute providing the penalty for burglary.

§2.7   COLLATERAL REFERENCE

This generic term indicates references to other works. Thus, an encyclopedia discussing the elements of a cause of action might include a collateral reference to the portion of a form book explaining how to draft a complaint involving the cause of action. A treatise might collaterally refer to a pertinent law review article. Collateral references can be great time-savers, subject to the following limitations: (1) Most commercial publishers do not refer to the works of competing publishers, and (2) some collateral references look useful but end up providing little or no new information.

§2.8   ANNOTATION

Generically, the term "annotation" refers to material (provided by the publisher) which explains, amplifies, or illustrates the text. The most common example of this use of the term is an annotated code. Annotations generally consist of casenotes, editorial explanations, collateral references, practice tips, and sample forms. The term is also used to refer to ALR annotations (see §5.22). Annotations may be valuable pointers, telling the researcher where else to look for additional material on the topic.

§2.9   BINDING

Most law books are hardcover volumes, intended to be retained permanently or for the long term. Reporters, encyclopedias, and digests are examples. Bound softcover volumes are less common and are generally intended to be retained for a short term. Advance legislative services are examples. An alternative to bound volumes is some form of ring or post binder with either loose pages or softcover pamphlets. These are commonly referred to as looseleafs. (See §2.13.)

§2.10   SINGLE VOLUMES AND SETS

Some law books consist of a single volume. Many treatises and topical works are examples. It is far more common, however, for individual volumes to be part of larger sets, ranging from two or three to hundreds of volumes. Codes, reporters, and encyclopedias are examples. Multivolume sets tend to be arranged either chronologically (reporters), numerically (codes), or alphabetically by topic (encyclopedias and digests).

§2.11   SUPPLEMENTATION

The single most troublesome problem with law books is timeliness. Because of constant change and development in the law, virtually all law books are or may be out of date by the time they are published. To replace thousands of hardcover volumes once or twice a year is economically impractical. Therefore, while some volumes (usually softcover) are intended to be replaced annually, most hardcover books are retained from year to year and kept up to date with an annual (or periodic) supplement. These supplements are of three types:

(1)   Softcover pamphlets, which stand next to the parent volume on the shelf. Many CEB practice works are examples.

(2)   Pocket parts, which fit inside a pocket in the back of the parent volume. Annotated codes are examples.

(3)   Hardcover supplements. These are not common. If used, more than one volume of the parent set may be

supplemented in the same hardcover supplement volume. These hardcover supplements may in turn be supplemented with pocket parts or softcover pamphlets. ALR2d and some elements of Shepard's citations are examples. This supplementation mechanism is the least efficient, inasmuch as the user must look at three places rather than the usual two.

As a general rule, supplements are cumulative, i.e., this year's pocket part or pamphlet replaces last year's. There are exceptions, however: a bound volume and a supplement issued in a prior year, for example, might be retained as a permanent historical record. When a new supplement is issued, the publisher usually includes filing instructions (see §2.18) indicating which prior supplements are to be replaced and which retained. Frequently, the cover of the supplement identifies the volumes and supplements the library should retain. Some examples of this practice are Shepard's (see §11.3), CALJIC and BAJI (see §4.23).

To gather the most current information available, a researcher should always check the most recent supplement. Because supplements are usually replaced at least annually, a book with a supplement more than a year old is suspect. Because many libraries keep replaced volumes, a researcher should always check the volume carefully. As a generally rule, if a section of the hardcover volume has no material in the supplement, the implication is that the bound volume is still correct. Many researchers check the supplement first, then the parent volume.

Although most law books are supplemented annually, a large set of books with individual supplements may be enhanced by additional semi-annual or quarterly pamphlets. Annotated federal codes (USCS and USCA) are examples. Thus, a researcher may need to check three locations to get a complete picture.

§2.12   ANNUAL REPLACEMENT VOLUMES

Some volumes (usually softcover) are intended to be used for a short period of time (usually one year) and are then replaced with a new version. Supplementation in the conventional sense is not required. Directories and unannotated codes are common examples. To the researcher, the obvious benefit, of course, is the need to look in only one location to find current information.

§2.13   LOOSELEAF FORMAT

True looseleaf publications lack separate supplements in the conventional sense. They use some variation of a ring or post binder and are kept up to date by replacement pages. With each new release (shipment of replacement pages), old pages are removed and new pages are inserted. Thus, a researcher needs to look in only one location to find current information. Looseleaf services (see §8.16) are updated frequently, often weekly or monthly. CCH publications are an example. On occasion, a looseleaf format is used, but updated replacement pages are issued less often, perhaps only annually. Several CEB practice works are examples.

Looseleafs have some drawbacks: (a) looseleafs tend to be more expensive because of the cost of frequent insertions, (b) page numbering is somewhat convoluted, and (c) the old version is lost unless the replaced pages are preserved. These problems are lessened by a variation called a pamphlet binder, which uses bound softcover pamphlets in the binder rather than separate loose pages. Individual pamphlets are more easily replaced than an entire volume, but there may be a corresponding loss in timeliness. A number of looseleaf publications provide additional pages periodically but do not remove or replace existing pages. Generally, these additional pages are called a supplement, printed on a different color paper, and are filed together at the front or back of the volume.

§2.14   SELECTIVELY REVISED VOLUMES

Because the law changes more rapidly in some areas than in others, not all individual volumes in a large set like an encyclopedia or code age at the same rate. For example, a ten-year old volume of the Military and Veterans Code with an annual supplement may be quite useful, while a five year old volume of the Probate Code may be hopelessly out-of-date. To address this problem, publishers often replace volumes in a large set as needed, frequently replacing one or two volumes with two or three. For the researcher, there are several consequences of this practice:

(1) Volume Numbers. In a consecutively numbered set, extra numbers may be inserted. Thus, for example, volume 9 may be replaced with volumes 9 and 9A.

(2) References to the Replaced Volume. References in other publications or companion volumes to the replaced volume will be incorrect. To alleviate this problem, publishers sometimes (a) provide parallel reference tables, linking the material in the replaced volume with that in the replacement volume, (b) retain the same section numbers in the replacement volume, or (c) provide updated references in the supplements of companion volumes.

(3) Index. The general index (for the set) will not accurately reflect the material and numbering in the replacement volume. Publishers generally address this problem by (a) providing an index for each volume or topic, or (b) correcting out-of-date references in the supplement to the general index.

(4) Publication Dates. The time frame of the material covered is not consistent from volume to volume, because the various books end and the supplements begin at staggered times.

§2.15   NEW EDITIONS AND SERIES

As with other reference books, out-of-date law books may be replaced with new editions, usually numbered (e.g., third edition) but sometimes called "revised" edition. The earlier edition is retired and often discarded, though it may be useful for historical research. Encyclopedias, treatises, and form books are examples of works that often have new editions.

A new series, in contrast, is a continuation rather than a replacement of the earlier series, which remains on the shelf and available for research. Fundamentally, only the name of the set has been changed, although publishers often use a new series as an opportunity to make cosmetic and stylistic changes. ALR annotations and case reporters are examples of new series. Thus, ALR3d is not replaced but continued in ALR4th and ALR5th, and California Reports 2d is not replaced but continued in California Reports 3d and California Reports 4th.

§2.16   ADVANCE SHEETS

While similar in appearance to supplements, advance sheets are distinct. With some exceptions (e.g. Shepard's), the term is generally reserved for softcover pamphlets published in connection with case reporters. They are designed not to supplement existing hardcover volumes, but to preview future hardcover volumes. The softcover pamphlets are issued frequently and intended to provide timely access to recent cases, without the delay occasioned by waiting for publication of a bound volume. Eventually several pamphlets are replaced with a permanent hardcover volume. Fortunately, most advance sheets use page numbers that are retained in the hardcover volume. This means that the citation of a case in the advance sheet will remain correct once the hardcover volume is published. (On California advance sheets, see §§5.6, 5.7.)

§2.17   CUMULATIONS

A few publications exist initially in a softcover format and are issued on a regular periodic basis. Often, successive issues replace one or more previous ones. For example, weekly or monthly issues may be cumulated quarterly. Eventually, usually annually, the softcover issues are replaced with a permanent bound volume. Legislative publications (like the journals of the California Assembly and Senate) are a common example.

§2.18   SHELVING AND FILING INSTRUCTIONS

When sending subscribers supplements or replacement volumes, legal publishers commonly enclose colored cards containing shelving or filing instructions. These cards explain what material may be discarded and what should be retained. They are most useful for updating looseleaf services, and, in the case of looseleafs, should be kept permanently in the binder as a way of checking for timeliness. Filing cards (or the covers of pamphlet supplements and pocket parts) often include customer service telephone and fax numbers. On occasion, the filing instructions contain a checklist of the volumes in the set.

§2.19   MICROFICHE

A variety of legal materials are available on microfilm or microfiche. Government documents, regulations, and newspapers are examples. A major microfiche vendor, the Law Library Microfilm Consortium [(808) 235-2200] publishes thousands of documents on microfiche, generally government publications and publications out of copyright. The following are illustrative:

USC
Statutes at Large
Digest of Public General Bills and Resolutions
The Congressional Record (and predecessors)
Public Papers of the Presidents
Weekly Compilation of Presidential Documents
Internal Revenue Cumulative Bulletin
National Reporter System (through 1916)
Various early California official and unofficial reporters
Various California agency documents (through 1979)

CHAPTER 3

THE LEGAL PROFESSION

This chapter provides basic information about the legal profession and identifies source material related to legal education, specialization, discipline, and organizations.

§3.1	Regulation of Law Practice	34
§3.2	State Bar of California	34
§3.3	State Bar Rules	35
§3.4	Local and Specialty Associations	36
§3.5	National Associations	37
§3.6	State Bar and ABA Sections	37
§3.7	Lawyer Directories	39
§3.8	Legal Ethics	40
§3.9	Continuing Legal Education	41
§3.10	Law Schools	41

---

§3.1   REGULATION OF LAW PRACTICE

Each state has a statewide bar association. Membership is either voluntary or mandatory (membership in the association is a prerequisite for practicing law in that state). Where membership is mandatory, as in California, the bar association is said to be integrated. In California, the statewide association is called the State Bar of California. (See §3.2.) The American Bar Association (ABA) and local and specialty associations are voluntary. (See §3.4.)

Most bar associations have subgroups, called committees or sections, which are special interest groups for various areas of practice or address issues of concern to the legal community. Sections generally publish newsletters and frequently support legislation of interest to their members. (On bar association sections, see §3.16)

The California Rules of Court and local rules govern practice before California courts. Federal rules govern practice before federal courts. (On rules of court, see §4.19 et seq.)

§3.2   STATE BAR OF CALIFORNIA

The State Bar of California is established by the California Constitution (Article VI, §9) and is governed by the State Bar Act (Business and Professions Code §6000 et seq.). All lawyers practicing law in California must be members. The State Bar has a Board of Governors (with both lawyer and public members) and an extensive professional staff which administers a variety of programs. The State Bar has specialty sections and standing committees. (On sections, see §3.6; on section newsletters, see §9.11.) Its major activities include: (1) admission to practice, (2) discipline, (3) specialization, and (4) client trust accounts.

Although the State Bar of California oversees the admission to practice and the discipline of lawyers, members of the bar in California are formally admitted to practice before California courts by the California Supreme Court, which also has authority to review disciplinary decisions of the State Bar Court. Admission to practice in federal courts in California is governed by those courts, which generally admit those who are admitted to practice in California courts.

The State Bar's Board of Legal Specialization publishes an annual directory, California Certified Legal Specialists. The board certifies legal specialists in:

(1) Bankruptcy
(2) Criminal law
(3) Family law
(4) Immigration and nationality
(5) Probate, estate planning and trust law
(6) Taxation
(7) Workers' compensation

The State Bar has offices in San Francisco [(415) 561-8200] and Los Angeles [(213) 580-5000].

§3.3   STATE BAR RULES

Various rules, collectively known as State Bar rules, govern the programs and functions of the State Bar of California. (For published sources, see §4.22.) The rules relate to the following topics:

(1) Rules and Regulations of the State Bar of California
(2) Rules of Professional Conduct
(3) Rules of procedure of the State Bar
(4) Admission to practice
(5) State Bar Court
(6) Mandatory fee arbitration programs and hearings
(7) Lawyer referral services
(8) Client security fund matters
(9) Interest-bearing trust accounts
(10) Law corporations
(11) Program for certifying legal specialists
(12) Meetings and records of the Board of Governors
(13) Minimum continuing legal education

(14) Commission on Judicial Nominee Evaluation
(15) Practical training of law students

§3.4   LOCAL AND SPECIALTY ASSOCIATIONS

There are many county, local, and specialty associations for lawyers and other legal professionals in California, including regional chapters of national associations. The State Bar's Office of Bar Relations [(415) 561-8200 ext. 7430] maintains a current list of local and specialty bar associations. Relevant information is also frequently available in lawyer directories. (On lawyer directories, see §3.7.) Many local bar associations publish membership directories, newsletters and magazines, sponsor continuing legal education programs, and provide other services for their members. The most prominent local and specialty associations include the following:

Alameda County Bar Association
Bar Association of San Francisco (BASF)
Beverly Hills Bar Association
California Academy of Appellate Lawyers
California Alliance of Paralegal Associations
California Attorneys for Criminal Justice
California District Attorneys Association
California Public Defenders Association
California Trial Lawyers Association (CTLA)
California Women Lawyers
Lawyers Club of Los Angeles
Lawyers Club of San Francisco
Los Angeles County Bar Association
Orange County Bar Association
San Diego County Bar Association
San Francisco Association of Legal Assistants
Santa Clara County Bar Association

§3.5   NATIONAL ASSOCIATIONS

There are national associations for legal professionals, many with state and local chapters in California. The Lawyer's Almanac (see §1.11) has an extensive list. The following are illustrative:

American Academy of Matrimonial Lawyers
American Association of Attorney-Certified Public Accountants
American Association of Law Librarians
American Bar Association (ABA): (312) 988-5000
American Board of Trial Advocates
American College of Real Estate Lawyers
American College of Trusts and Estates Attorneys
Association of Business Trial Lawyers
Association of Defense Counsel
Association of Defense Trial Attorneys
Association of Legal Administrators
Association of Trial Lawyers of America (ATLA)
Defense Research Institute
Federation of Insurance and Corporate Counsel
International Association of Defense Counsel
Maritime Law Association of the United States
National Assn of Legal Assistants
National Federation of Paralegal Associations

§3.6   STATE BAR AND ABA SECTIONS

The State Bar of California has the following sections:

Antitrust & Trade Regulation
Business Law
Criminal Law
Environmental Law
Estate Planning, Trust & Probate
Family Law
General Practice
Intellectual Property
International Law
Labor & Employment Law
Law Practice Management

Legal Services
Litigation
Public Law
Real Property Law
Taxation
Workers' Compensation

The ABA has the following sections and divisions:

Administrative Law & Regulatory Practice
Air and Space Law
Antitrust Law
Business Law
Communications Law
Construction Industry
Criminal Justice
Entertainment and Sports Industries
Family Law
Franchising
General Practice
Health Law
Individual Rights & Responsibilities
International Law & Practice
Judicial Administration Division
Labor & Employment Law
Law Practice Management
Legal Education & Admissions to the Bar
Litigation
Natural Resources, Energy & Environmental Law
Patent, Trademark & Copyright Law
Public Contract Law
Public Utility Law
Real Property, Probate & Trust Law
Science & Technology
Taxation
Tort & Insurance Practice
Urban, State & Local Government Law

§3.7   LAWYER DIRECTORIES

There are dozens of directories of lawyers, both general and specialized, including organization membership directories. Directories often include court and government information as well as information about lawyers, professional associations, and vendors of legal services. The following are illustrative:

California Lawyers; semi-annual; Daily Journal Corporation; softcover; includes listings for lawyers, courts, bar associations, law schools, court reporters, arbitrators, court reporters, expert witnesses, private judges, federal, state, and local government.

California Legal Directory; annual; Legal Directories Publishing Company; hardcover (blue).

Parker Directory of California Attorneys; annual; Parker Publications; softcover; two volumes; semi-annual update of volume I (attorney and firm listings); volume II includes information about state and federal offices, courts, bar associations, court reporters, certified specialists, and expert witnesses.

California Certified Legal Specialists; annual; State Bar of California, Board of Legal Specialization.

Directory of California Corporate Counsel; 1987; State Bar of California, Business Law Section.

Directory of Attorneys - Los Angeles and Orange Counties; Daily Journal Corporation.

Directory of San Francisco Attorneys; annual; Bar Association of California.

Dispute Resolution Directory: Programs and Resources in California; State Bar of California, Office of Legal Services; identifies dispute resolution programs in California for low and moderate income people.

Intellectual Property Directory; 1993; The Recorder and The American Lawyer; identifies California firms practicing in intellectual property and related fields.

Martindale Hubbell Law Directory; annual; R.R. Bowker; hardcover; 13 volumes; alphabetical by state; available on CD-ROM from Bowker Electronic Publishing and online from Lexis.

Martindale Hubbell International Law Directory; R.R. Bowker; annual; hardcover; one volume; Canadian and international lawyers; available on CD-ROM from Bowker Electronic Publishing and online from Lexis.

West's Legal Directory; online; West Publishing Company.

§3.8   LEGAL ETHICS

Standards of professional conduct for California lawyers are set forth in the Rules of Professional Conduct of the State Bar of California. (For published sources for the Rules of Professional Conduct, see §4.22.) Violation of these requirements may result in disciplinary proceedings leading to private or public reproval, suspension, or disbarment. The following resources are available:

California Compendium on Professional Responsibility; State Bar of California; looseleaf (black); three volumes; annual update; includes a comprehensive subject matter index, the Rules of Professional Conduct, various other State Bar rules, advisory ethics opinions of the State Bar's Standing Committee on Professional Responsibility and Conduct and the ethics committees of the Bar Association of San Francisco, the Los Angeles County Bar Association and the San Diego County Bar Association. The State Bar's advisory ethics opinions are available online from Westlaw (CALS-EO database).

Ethics Hotliner; State Bar of California; newsletter; quarterly; summary of recent advisory ethics opinions; statutory and case law highlights; proposed changes in the Rules of Professional Conduct. Ethics Hotline: (800) 238-4427.

California State Bar Court Reporter; State Bar of California; three volumes; quarterly update; full text of published opinions of the State Bar Court Review Department.

Martindale Hubbell has announced a Universal Lawyer Numbering System which assigns each lawyer a unique identification number to be used primarily for tracking disciplinary action by state bar associations.

§3.9   CONTINUING LEGAL EDUCATION

Many states, including California, require lawyers to satisfy continuing education requirements as a condition of practice. This requirement is generally known as MCLE for mandatory (or minimum) continuing legal education. In California, the general requirement is 36 hours of continuing education over a three year period. Generally, the requirement may be satisfied by attending seminars, viewing videotapes, or listening to audiotapes, which have been approved by the State Bar of California. CLE providers prepare written program materials. (See §13.10.)

§3.10   LAW SCHOOLS

California has over fifty law schools. They are often listed in lawyer directories, including California Lawyers, published by the Daily Journal Corporation. (On lawyer directories, see §3.7.) Most Law schools publish one or more law reviews. (On law reviews, see §9.6 et seq.) (On law school texts, see §9.4.)

CHAPTER 4

THE JUDICIAL BRANCH

This chapter introduces the structure and functions of the judicial branch, and provides information about rules, forms, and jury instructions.

§4.1	In General	44
§4.2	Jurisdiction	44
§4.3	Trial and Appellate Courts	46
§4.4	Court Records and Fees	47
§4.5	Federal Judicial System	48
§4.6	California Judicial System	50
§4.7	Supreme Court	51
§4.8	Courts of Appeal	52
§4.9	Superior Courts	53
§4.10	Municipal and Justice Courts	54
§4.11	Judicial Council	54
§4.12	Reporter of Decisions	55
§4.13	Law Revision Commission	56
§4.14	Commission on Judicial Appointments	56
§4.15	Commission on Judicial Performance	57
§4.16	California Judges Association	57
§4.17	Center for Judicial Education and Research	57
§4.18	Judicial Council Forms	58
§4.19	California Rules of Court	59
§4.20	Local Court Rules and Forms	61
§4.21	Federal Court Rules and Forms	61
§4.22	Published Rules	62
§4.23	Jury Instructions	64
§4.24	Court and Judges Directories	65

---

§4.1   IN GENERAL

The judicial branch of government is concerned with the administration of justice and the resolution of disputes between litigants. It consists of judges, exercising authority in court, and judicial agencies. The federal court system and the court systems in the fifty states are separate entities, each acting in its own geographical area and governed by its own statutes and rules.   (On matters of state and federal law, see §1.4.) Nevertheless, their activities sometimes intersect:

(1)   A single transaction may have consequences in more than one jurisdiction, e.g., the same act may be a crime under both state and federal law and thus may be prosecuted is two proceedings with two sentences.

(2)   Decisions of state courts involving rights claimed under the United States Constitution or under a federal statute may be reviewed by the United States Supreme Court.

§4.2   JURISDICTION

The concept of jurisdiction is both complex and amorphous. Vastly simplified, it has the following components:

(1)   Geographical Jurisdiction. The term "jurisdiction" is commonly used to refer to the geographical area in which a court has authority. While the authority of every court is subject to geographical limits, the geographical use of the term is usually used to refer to the highest courts of the states and, by extension, to the states themselves. Thus, "in this jurisdiction" almost always means "in this state."

(2)   Personal Jurisdiction (In Personam Jurisdiction). A court's authority to compel a person to do or refrain from doing an act. Personal jurisdiction is generally based on some connection with the state in which the court sits, for example, residing in the state, being

personally present in the state, or engaging in certain conduct in the state.

(3) <u>Jurisdiction Over Property (In Rem Jurisdiction)</u>. A court's authority over property physically present within the geographical jurisdiction of the court, even in the absence of personal jurisdiction over persons interested in the property. In rem jurisdiction, for example, allows a court to determine an action to quiet title to property, even though all possible claimants are not present.

(4) <u>Subject Matter Jurisdiction</u>. A court's authority to act based on the subject matter of a dispute. Typically, a court's jurisdiction is limited to certain kinds of cases, by the amount of money in controversy, or by the relief requested.

(5) <u>Limited or Special Jurisdiction</u>. The court has subject matter jurisdiction only in specified areas or amounts. A court which has jurisdiction only if the amount in controversy is under a given dollar amount, e.g., $5000, is a court of limited jurisdiction.

(6) <u>General Jurisdiction</u>. The court has subject matter jurisdiction over all cases arising within its geographical boundaries, except where jurisdiction is exclusively reserved to other courts.

(7) <u>Exclusive Jurisdiction</u>. Only one court has authority to act is a given situation.

(8) <u>Concurrent Jurisdiction</u>. More than one court has authority to act in a given situation.

(9) <u>Original Jurisdiction</u>. The first court with authority to hear a case has original jurisdiction over the case. The term generally refers to the trial court.

(10) <u>Appellate Jurisdiction</u>. The authority to hear appeals from lower courts.

If a court lacks jurisdiction, its act may be void or voidable: either the act is an invalid act which may not become valid (void) or is a valid act which may become invalid if a party chooses to challenge it (voidable).

§4.3   TRIAL AND APPELLATE COURTS

In the United States, courts are commonly arranged in a three-tier structure, consisting of trial courts and two levels of appellate courts. Both the federal courts and the California courts use this model, as do many other states. Some states, however, lack the second tier. In addition, terminology is not consistent from state to state. The district court may be a trial court in one state and an appellate court in another. The three-tier system gives rise to the expressions "higher court" and "lower court."

(1) First Tier. The first tier consists of trial courts, both courts of limited jurisdiction and courts of general jurisdiction. (On jurisdiction, see §4.2.) Trial courts hear evidence, determine the facts, and make an initial determination or ruling. Sometimes they review decisions of administrative agencies.

The trial court of general jurisdiction is often called the superior court, the circuit court, the district court, or the court of common pleas. Trial courts of limited jurisdiction are often called the municipal court, the justice court, or the county court. The family court, the juvenile court, and the probate court may either be separate courts or divisions of the trial court of general jurisdiction. Traffic court is generally a division of the trial court of limited jurisdiction. Often, trial courts sit in separate criminal and civil divisions.

In the federal system, the general trial court is the United States District Court, which sits in geographical districts throughout the country (see §4.5). Limited trial courts include the United States Tax Court and the United States Claims Court. In California, the general trial court is the Superior Court (see §4.9). Limited trial courts are the municipal court and the justice court (see §4.10).

(2) <u>Second Tier</u>. The second tier consists of intermediate appellate courts, which generally review the decisions of trial courts to correct errors of law. Usually, appellate courts do not determine the facts (and thus, have no need to hear evidence or see witnesses). Their review is generally limited to the record (pleadings; documents; transcripts). Their job is to determine whether the trial court properly applied the correct legal principles to the facts.

Most frequently, the intermediate appellate court is called the court of appeal, the district court of appeal or the circuit court of appeal. In the federal system, this court is the United States Circuit Court of Appeal, which sits in geographical circuits throughout the country (see §4.5). In California, the intermediate appellate court is the Court of Appeal, which sits in geographical districts (see §4.8).

(3) <u>Third Tier</u>. The third tier consists of the highest appellate court, called the court of last resort. This court reviews decisions of the intermediate appellate court or the trial court.

The highest court is usually called the supreme court, though there are exceptions: In New York state, for example, the trial court of general jurisdiction is the supreme court and the highest court is the court of appeal. In the federal system, this is the United States Supreme Court (see §4.5). In California, this is the Supreme Court of California (see §4.7).

§4.4   TRIAL COURT RECORDS AND FEES

<u>Fees</u>. Trial court filing fees are frequently published in litigation practice works, newspapers, and court directories (see §4.2). The annual California Courts Directory and Fee Schedule, published by the Association of Municipal Court Clerks, is widely available. The clerk's office often has a posted schedule as well. Because fees are subject to change, the best practice in an unfamiliar county is to call the clerk of the court to verify the fee.

Case Files. Pending and recent case files are available for inspection and copying (for a hefty charge) in the clerk's office. Older files may be stored off-site, but may be recovered with sufficient patience. Files are arranged by case number, which must be discovered in indexes and tables, like the plaintiff-defendant table, linking the names of the parties and other information with the case number. Typically, information about younger cases is available on computer, while information about older cases is stored on microfiche, microfilm, or paper. Computer systems vary from court to court, but may allow searching by name (party or attorney), case number, or date, and reveal the contents of the case file and the stage reached in litigation.

Services. State and federal trial court record searches are often performed by information brokers (see §1.7), and online services are beginning to include computerized finding aids. For example, court records in four of the state's largest counties are available on Lexis in the CAL library (see §12.5).

§4.5   THE FEDERAL JUDICIAL SYSTEM

The judicial branch of government in the federal system is established by the United States Constitution and by Title 28 of the United States Code (28 USC). It consists of general and specialized trial courts, intermediate appellate courts and a court of last resort. Its various elements include the following:

(1) District Court. The states and territories are grouped into approximately 100 geographical judicial districts. Districts do not cross state lines (except that those parts of Yellowstone National Park in Idaho and Montana are within the District of Wyoming). An entire state may constitute a single district (e.g., the District of Oregon) or may be divided into two, three or four districts (e.g., the Eastern and Western districts of Washington). In each judicial districts, the trial court of general jurisdiction is the United States District Court. The correct terminology is the United States District Court for the [Northern, Southern, Eastern, Western, Central, Middle] District of [state]. (See 28 USC §81 et seq.)

California includes the Northern District, the Eastern District, the Central District, and the Southern District. The Northern District hold regular sessions in Eureka, Oakland, San Francisco, and San Jose. The Eastern District holds regular sessions in Fresno, Redding, and Sacramento. The Central District hold regular sessions in Los Angeles and Santa Ana. The Southern District holds regular sessions in San Diego.

(2) Specialized Trial Courts. There are a number of judicial and administrative tribunals that serve as trial courts of special jurisdiction, including:

  (a) U.S. Claims Court (See 28 USC §171 et seq.)
  (b) Court of International Trade (See 28 USC §251 et seq.)
  (c) U.S. International Trade Commission
  (d) Merit System Protection Board
  (e) Tax Court
  (f) Federal Trade Commission
  (g) National Labor Relations Board

(3) Court of Appeals. The nation is also divided into twelve geographical judicial circuits. The states and territories are apportioned among eleven numbered circuits geographically. The twelfth circuit, consisting of Washington, D.C., is called the District of Columbia Circuit. A thirteenth circuit, called the Federal Circuit, is nationwide. In each judicial circuit, the appellate court of general jurisdiction is the United States Court of Appeals. The correct terminology is the United States Court of Appeals for the [number] Circuit. The court hears appeals from district courts within its circuit. California is part of the Ninth Circuit. The court holds regular sessions in San Francisco, Los Angeles, Portland, and Seattle. (See 28 USC §41 et seq.)

(4) Bankruptcy Court. Bankruptcy judges in each district comprise a unit of the district court known as the bankruptcy court for the district. The Circuit designates bankruptcy judges to hear appeals, often in a group called the Bankruptcy Appellate Panel. (See 28 USC §151 et seq.)

(5) Specialized Appellate Courts. The Court of Appeals for the Federal Circuit is an appellate court of limited jurisdiction, hearing appeals in customs and patent cases and appeals from the U.S. Claims Court, the Court of International Trade, the U.S.

International Trade Commission, and the Merit System Protection Board. Other specialized federal appellate courts include The Temporary Emergency Court of Appeals, and the United States Court of Military Appeals.

(6) <u>Supreme Court</u>. The highest federal court, of course, is the United States Supreme Court, composed of the Chief Justice of the United States and eight associate justices. It hears appeals from the thirteen circuits and from the courts of last resort in the various states. (See 28 USC §1 et seq.)

(7) <u>Federal Judicial Agencies</u>. Among the various federal judicial agencies are the following:

(a) Judicial Conference of the United States
(b) Federal Judicial Center
(c) Administrative Office of the United States Courts
(d) Judicial Panel on Multidistrict Litigation
(e) Judicial Council in each circuit
(f) Judicial Conference of each circuit

§4.6   THE CALIFORNIA JUDICIAL SYSTEM

The judicial branch of government in California is established by Article VI of the California Constitution, which vests judicial power in the Supreme Court, the Courts of Appeal, superior courts, municipal courts, and justice courts. Judicial administration is provided by the following agencies:

(1) The Judicial Council, which supervises the operation of the courts and adopts statewide rules and forms. (See §4.11.)

(2) The Commission of Judicial Appointments, which confirms gubernatorial appointments to appellate courts. (See §4.14.)

(3) The Commission on Judicial Performance, which sanctions judges for misconduct or disability. (See §4.15.)

In 1991, there were 214 courts in California and 1555 authorized judgeships.

§4.7   SUPREME COURT

California's highest court is the Supreme Court, which consists of a chief justice and six associate justices. The members of the court are appointed by the Governor and must be confirmed by the Commission on Judicial Appointments (see §4.14). They are then confirmed by the electorate and serve for twelve year terms. To be qualified for appointment, a person must be a California attorney or have served as the judge of a court of record for the ten years immediately preceding the appointment. (See Cal. Const., Art. VI, §2; Government Code §68801 et seq.)

The court is located in San Francisco, though its official home is in Sacramento. (Government Code 1060.) It also regularly hears cases in Los Angeles and Sacramento. Generally, all seven justices participate in each case. The court has the following jurisdiction:

(1)   Discretionary review of decisions of the Courts of Appeal. The court may decide all issues in a case or select specific issues for review. (Cal. Const., Art. VI, §12; California Rules of Court, Rule 28 et seq.) The court also has authority to transfer a case from the Court of Appeal to itself without waiting for the Court of Appeal to issue a decision.

(2)   Mandatory review of cases in which the trial court imposes the death penalty. (Cal. Const., Art. VI, §11.) Death penalty cases are appealed directly to the Supreme Court without review in the Court of Appeal.

(3)   Original jurisdiction in proceedings for mandamus, certiorari, prohibition, and habeas corpus. (Cal. Const., Art. VI, §10.)

(4)   Review of decisions of the Public Utilities Commission.

(5) Review of disciplinary recommendations of the Commission of Judicial Performance (see §4.15) and the State Bar Court.

The Supreme Court has issued the following explanatory booklets:

(1) Supreme Court Policies Regarding Cases Arising from Judgments of Death.

(2) Internal Operating Practices and Procedures of the Supreme Court of California (1989 Revision).

§4.8   COURTS OF APPEAL

California's intermediate appellate courts, the Courts of Appeal, were established by Constitutional amendment in 1904. They now consist of six appellate districts, each of which is composed of divisions. Generally, cases are heard by a three-judge panel. Justices are appointed by the Governor and confirmed by the Commission on Judicial Appointments (see §4.14). They are then confirmed by the electorate and serve for twelve year terms. (See Cal. Const., Art. VI, §3; Government Code §69101 et seq.) The appellate districts are:

(1) First District: San Francisco
(2) Second District: Los Angeles
(3) Third District: Sacramento
(4) Fourth District: San Diego
(5) Fifth District: Fresno
(6) Sixth District: San Jose

The court has the following jurisdiction:

(1) Appellate jurisdiction where the superior courts have original jurisdiction and where statute so provides.

(2) Original jurisdiction in proceedings for mandamus, certiorari, prohibition, and habeas corpus.

The opinions of the Courts of Appeal are selectively published. (See §5.9.) In 1991, there were 88 justices, sitting in 18 divisions.

§4.9 SUPERIOR COURTS

The Superior Court is the trial court of general jurisdiction, with jurisdiction over all matters in which trial jurisdiction is not given by statute to another court. Each of California's 58 counties has a superior court. Judges serve six year terms and are elected by the voters of the county. (See Cal. Const., Art. VI, §§4, 10; Government Code §69501 et seq.) The court has the following jurisdiction:

(1) Probate, juvenile, adoption, competency and domestic relations. Often, there are separate branches or divisions of the court for these specialized areas. Thus, for example, the term "probate court" refers not to a separate court, but to the superior court exercising probate jurisdiction.

(2) Felony cases.

(3) Civil matters where the amount in controversy is over the jurisdictional limit for municipal and justice courts ($25,000).

(4) Cases seeking special relief, e.g., injunctive or declaratory relief.

The appellate department of the Superior Court acts as an appellate court for appeals from the municipal and justice court (see §4.10). In 1991, there were 789 superior court judges and 116 commissioners and referees.

§4.10   MUNICIPAL AND JUSTICE COURTS

There are two trial courts of limited jurisdiction, the municipal court and the justice court. Originally, these courts were separately operated. Today, though separate, their operation and jurisdiction is generally the same. The state is divided into judicial districts. The municipal court sits in districts with a population over 40,000. The justice court sits in districts with a population less than 40,000. The term for both courts is six years. (See Cal. Const., Art. VI, §§5, 11; Government Code §71001 et seq.) The courts have the following jurisdiction:

(1) Misdemeanor and infraction cases.

(2) Civil matters (not otherwise within the exclusive jurisdiction of the superior court) in which the amount in controversy is less than $25,000.

(3) Small claims jurisdiction (the amount in controversy is less than $5000).

Judges of the municipal and justice courts also act as magistrates, presiding over preliminary hearings in felony cases. In 1991, there were 92 municipal courts, with 614 judges and 134 commissioners and referees, and 57 justice courts, each with a single judge.

§4.11   JUDICIAL COUNCIL

The Judicial Council of California was established in 1926. It is the policy-making and rule-making body for the California courts, and is composed of variously appointed judges, lawyers, legislators, and advisory members. The Chief Justice of the California Supreme Court is the Chairperson of the Judicial Council. (See Cal. Const., Art. VI, §6; Government Code §68500 et seq.; California Rules of Court, Rule 990 et seq.) The Council does the following:

(1) Surveys judicial business, and makes recommendations to the courts, the Governor, and the Legislature. (Cal. Const., Art. VI, §6.)

(2) Adopts rules for court administration, practice and procedure. (Cal. Const., Art. VI, §6.) Adopts forms. (See California Rules of Court, Rules 982 et seq.) (On rules, see §4.19; on forms, see §4.18.)

(3) Publishes an annual report in two softcover volumes (Report to the Governor and the Legislature and Judicial Statistics).

(4) Appoints advisory committees composed of judges, lawyers, and experts in various fields.

The Administrative Office of the Courts (AOC), under the direction of the Administrative Director of the Courts, is the staff agency of the Judicial Council and carries out its actions and policies. (See California Rules of Court, Rules 990 et seq.) The AOC publishes (1) an annual statistical report concerning the state's judicial business, and (2) a monthly newsletter providing information about court activities, personnel, rules, and forms.

§4.12   REPORTER OF DECISIONS

The State of California contracts with a private publisher (Bancroft Whitney) to publish the official reports of the California courts (see §5.4). The Reporter of Decisions supervises the publication and provides editorial review of the California official reports, consisting of (1) California Reports (decisions of the California Supreme Court), and (2) California Appellate Reports (decisions of the California Courts of Appeal and the appellate department of the superior court). The reporter is appointed by the Supreme Court and has a small staff. (See Government Code §68900 et seq.)

§4.13   LAW REVISION COMMISSION

The California Law Revision Commission was formed in 1953. Its purposes are to study California law for errors and defects and to recommend corrective legislation. The Commission studies those topics authorized by the Legislature and drafts recommended statutes. Its work is of high quality and its recommendations are frequently adopted by the Legislature. As an illustration, the Legislature's extensive revision of the Probate Code in the 1980s was the result of a number of Commission recommendations. The Commission consists of a member of the Senate, a member of the Assembly, the Legislative Counsel, and seven members appointed by the Governor. (See generally Government Code §8280 et seq.)

The Commission publishes its recommendations and an annual report in softcover pamphlets (light blue) which are cumulated in hardcover volumes. Each recommendation consists of a report, the text of proposed statutes, and comments for each statute for which the Commission recommends enactment, amendment, or repeal. The comments are extremely valuable in assessing the purpose and intent of the legislation, and are frequently included as annotations to the annotated codes. (On legislative intent, see §6.13; on annotated codes, see §7.6.)

Citation: Volume / Title / Page / Year
          20 Cal. L. Revision Comm'n Reports 2001 (1990).

§4.14   COMMISSION ON JUDICIAL APPOINTMENTS

Justices of the California Supreme Court and Courts of Appeal are appointed by the Governor. The Commission on Judicial Appointments has the authority to confirm or deny these appointments. It does so after conducting public hearings. The commission consists of (1) the Chief Justice, (2) the Attorney General, and (3) for Court of Appeal nominations, the senior presiding justice of the Court of Appeal for that district, and for Supreme Court nominations, the senior presiding justice of the Courts of Appeal. (See Cal. Const., Art. VI, §§7, 16.)

§4.15   COMMISSION ON JUDICIAL PERFORMANCE

The Commission on Judicial Performance consists of nine members, and includes judges, lawyers, and public members. The commission and it staff investigate complaints about judicial misconduct or disability. The commission may issue a confidential advisory letter, a private admonishment, or a public reproval and may recommend the censure, removal, or retirement of a judge. Recommendations are determined by a tribunal of judges of the Court of Appeal selected by lot. (See Cal. Const., Art. VI, §§8, 18; Government Code §68701 et seq.; California Rules of Court, Rule 901 et seq.)

§4.16   CALIFORNIA JUDGES ASSOCIATION

The California Judges Association (CJA) is a voluntary association of California judges. Its predecessor association was formed in response to a California Supreme Court opinion in 1929, holding that a judge is not a member of the state bar and not subject to its disciplinary rules. The association has adopted the Code of Judicial Conduct, which is published as an appendix to the California Rules of Court. The association is also active in judicial education. Its tax-exempt fund-raising arm is the California Judges Foundation.

§4.17   CENTER FOR JUDICIAL EDUCATION AND RESEARCH

The California Center for Judicial Education and Research (CJER) is a joint enterprise of the Judicial Council and the California Judges Association. It provides orientation and continuing education programs for judges. CJER also publishes guides for judges in a series called California Judges Benchbook. (See §10.9.)

§4.18   JUDICIAL COUNCIL FORMS

One of the most important functions of the Judicial Council (see §4.11) is to promulgate court forms. Forms are either mandatory ("adopted") or optional ("approved"). Generally, new forms and changes in existing forms are effective on January 1st or July 1st. Forms have been adopted or approved in the following areas:

General legal forms	No. 982(a)(1) et seq.
Pleading forms	No. 982.1(1) et seq.
Wage Garnishment	No. 982.5(1) et seq.
Family Law - General Practice	No. 1281 et seq.
Family Law - Joinder	No. 1291-10 et seq.
Family Law - Discovery	No. 1292.10 et seq.
Family Law - Summary Dissolution	No. 1295.10 et seq.
Family Law - Domestic Violence	No. 1295.90 et seq.
Family Law - Parentage	No. 1986.60 et seq.
Family Law - Expedited Child Support	No. 1297 et seq.
Facsimile Transmission	No. 2011.
Abortion	AB-100 et seq.
Attachment	AT-105 et seq.
Civil Harassment	CH-100 et seq.
Claim and Delivery	CD-100 et seq.
Enforcement of Judgment	EJ-100 et seq.
Form Interrogatories	FI-100 et seq.
Decedents' Estates	DE-110 et seq.
Guardianships and Conservatorships	GC-020 et seq.
Juvenile	JV-100 et seq.
Delay Reduction	DR-100 et seq.
Small Claims	SC-100 et seq.
Transitional Housing Misconduct	TH-100 et seq.
Miscellaneous	MC-010 et seq.

Judicial Council forms are available from court clerks and in the following publications:

(1)   Bancroft Whitney Judicial Council Forms Manual; Bancroft Whitney; softcover; one volume; oversize.

(2)   California Judicial Council Forms Manual; CEB; looseleaf; one volume.

(3)   Judicial Council Forms; Matthew Bender; two volumes; sold as part of California Forms of Pleading and Practice.

(4)   California Judicial Council Forms; West; softcover; one volume; pamphlet with detachable pages.

Judicial Council forms are also available by fax from Probus Research, a San Francisco court records research and retrieval firm.   Fax number: (415) 553-8077.   Computerized forms are available from CEB, Martin Dean's Essential Forms, and Legal Solutions.   (See §12.2.)

§4.19   CALIFORNIA RULES OF COURT

The California Rules of Court are adopted by the Judicial Council (see §4.11). Changes are generally effective January 1st or July 1st, though rules may be adopted, amended, or repealed at any time. The rules are arranged in the following way:

Title 1   Appellate Rules (1 et seq.)

Division I   Rules Relating to the Supreme Court and Courts of Appeal (1 et seq.)

Division II   Rules on Appeal to the Superior Court (101 et seq.)

Title 2   Pretrial and Trial Rules (201 et seq.)

Division I   Rules for the Superior Courts (201 et seq.)
Division II   Civil Law and Motion Rules (301 et seq.)
Division III   Sentencing Rules for the Superior Courts (401 et seq.)
Division IV   Rules for the Municipal Courts (501 et seq.)
Division V   Rules Relating to Justice Courts (701 et seq.)
Division VI   Miscellaneous Rules for Trial Courts (801 et seq.)

Title 3   Miscellaneous Rules (901 et seq.)

    Division I   Rules for Censure, Removal, Retirement and Private Admonishment of Judges (901 et seq.)

    Division II   Rules Relating to Attorney Admission and Disciplinary Proceedings and Review of State Bar Proceedings (951 et seq.)

    Division III   Rules for Publication of Appellate Opinions (976 et seq.)

    Division IV   General Rules Applicable to All Courts (980 et seq.)

    Division V   Rules Relating to the Administrative Director of the Courts and the Administrative Office of the Courts (990 et seq.)

    Division VI   Rules Relating to the Courts' Automation/Information Systems (1010 et seq.)

Title 4   Special Rules for Trial Courts (1201 et seq.)

    Division I   Family Law Rules (1201 et seq.)

    Division Ia   Juvenile Court Rules (1400 et seq.)

    Division II   Rules for Coordination of Civil Actions Commenced in Different Trial Courts (1501 et seq.)

    Division III   Judicial Arbitration Rules for Civil Cases (1600 et seq.)

    Division IV   Rules for Small Claims Actions (1701 et seq.)

    Division V   Delay Reduction Rules for Volunteer Trial Courts (1901 et seq.)

    Division VI   Rules for Fax is Pilot Project Counties (2001 et seq.)

Appendix

    Division I   Standards of Judicial Administration Recommended by the Judicial Council

    Division II   Code of Judicial Conduct

    Division V   Age Increase Factor Table

    Division VI   Discretionary Child Support

§4.20   LOCAL COURT RULES AND FORMS

While all courts in California are subject to the applicable provisions of the California Rules of Court, each local court is free to adopt rules and forms governing local court practice, to the extent not inconsistent with the statewide rules. All counties are required to either publish their own local rules or designate a private publisher to do so. Also, copies of the local rules must be available at the county clerk's office. (California Rules of Court, Rule 981.) Local rules generally cover these areas: law and motion; settlement conferences; arbitration; jury; family law; probate. In addition to superior court rules, there may be separate rules for municipal and justice courts.

The six districts of the Court of Appeal have each adopted local rules and internal operating practices and procedures.

The consequences of being unfamiliar with local rules can be catastrophic for both lawyer and client. Thus, although published rules are available, the only safe course in an unfamiliar area is to call the clerk of the court to determine local practice.

Selected forms in local Bay Area courts are available by fax from Probus Research, a San Francisco court records research and retrieval firm. Fax number: (415) 553-8077.

§4.21   FEDERAL COURT RULES AND FORMS

Federal courts are subject to the following rules which apply nationwide and which are published in annotated versions as part of the annotated federal code (USCS and USCA) (see §7.4):

(1)   Federal Rules of Civil Procedure
(2)   Federal Rules of Criminal Procedure
(3)   Federal Rules of Evidence
(4)   Federal Rules of Appellate Procedure

Each federal district and circuit may adopt local rules and forms. Frequently separate bankruptcy rules are also adopted. In

California, there are rules for the Ninth Circuit (with separate rules for the Bankruptcy Appellate Panel) and distinct rules for the Central, Eastern, Northern, and Southern Districts (with separate Bankruptcy Court rules). Local federal rules generally cover these areas: civil; criminal; admiralty; magistrates; jurors; arbitration. Sometimes the rules or appendixes include local forms or fee schedules.

Selected federal court forms are available by fax from Probus Research, a San Francisco court records research and retrieval firm. Fax number: (415) 553-8077.

§4.22   PUBLISHED RULES

Federal, state, and local court rules are available from commercial publishers in countless combinations and permutations. The most common include the following:

California Official Reports Advance Sheets.   Changes in the California Rules of Court and the local rules of the districts of the Courts of Appeal are published in the California Official Reports Advance Sheet pamphlets (tab number 5 in the green pages). (See §5.6.)

Deering's California Rules of Court; Bancroft Whitney; hardcover (maroon); three volumes; annual pocket part supplements. These volumes, an element of Deering's California Codes Annotated, are an annotated treatment of the California Rules of Court (in two volumes) and the State Bar rules (in one volume). (On Deering's, see §7.6.)

California Rules of Court, State; annual edition; West; softcover; one volume. Includes: California Rules of Court; local rules of the Courts of Appeal; State Bar rules.

California Rules of Court, Federal; annual edition; West; softcover; one volume. Includes: Federal Rules of Appellate Procedure; Ninth Circuit Rules (including bankruptcy); local rules of the four federal court districts within California.

Daily Journal Court Rules Service. This set publishes federal, state, and local rules for California and federal courts in two parts: (1) Court Rules for Northern California, and (2) Court Rules for Southern California. Each part consists of 7 looseleaf volumes updated monthly, arranged alphabetically by county. The Daily Journal Corporation also publishes rules for the U.S. Central District and Ninth Circuit and local rules for eleven selected counties in single volumes, either in softcover or looseleaf format.

Recorder Rules Service; looseleaf volumes; San Francisco County Rules Service; Alameda County Rules Service.

Metropolitan News Company [(213) 628-4384]; separate pamphlet binders for fourteen larger counties; two binders of federal rules.

California Local Rules of Court, San Francisco Bay Area Edition; annual replacement; Book Publishing Company [(800) 737-7881]; softcover; one volume; monthly looseleaf supplement; local rules from eleven Bay Area Counties.

Lexis, CAL library; text of California Rules of Court, history information, and cross references from Deering's California Codes Annotated.

California Local Probate Rules; annual edition; CEB; softcover; one volume.

Federal Local Court Rules, Civil and Admiralty Proceedings; Clark Boardman Callaghan; looseleaf.

Federal Agency Rules; Rules Service Company [(301) 424-9402]; includes Federal Communications Commission, Interstate Commerce Commission, Copyright Office, Patent and Trademark, Federal Aviation Administration, United States Court of International Trade, United States Tax Court, United States Claims Court.

§4.23   JURY INSTRUCTIONS

California's standard jury instructions are prepared by committees of the Superior Court of Los Angeles County. They are published in two sets:

(1)   CALJIC: California Jury Instructions - Criminal (5th edition); West; hardcover (blue); two volumes; semi-annual pocket parts.
Citation: CALJIC (5th ed); CALJIC [number of instruction].

(2)   BAJI (Book of Approved Jury Instructions); California Jury Instructions - Civil (7th edition); 1986; West; hardcover (maroon); two volumes; semi-annual pocket parts.
Citation: BAJI (7th ed); BAJI [number of instruction].

Each set includes the text of hundreds of instructions, accompanied by extensive use notes, comments, and citations to relevant statutes, cases, and commentaries. Each set also has (1) a detailed table of contents, (2) a table of cases, (3) a table of statutes, (4) a parallel reference table (linking current instruction numbers to numbers in previous edition) and (5) an index.

CALJIC has appendices relating to (1) findings necessary for special circumstances, enhancement of sentence, or denial of probation, (2) definitions of "reasonable doubt," and (3) lesser included and lesser related offenses. BAJI has appendices relating to (1) life expectancy, (2) present value, (3) rebuttable presumptions in civil cases, and (4) special verdicts.

The text of the instructions is available in two additional formats from West:

(1)   Looseleaf instructions in a format ready for filing: BAJI Forms and CALJIC Forms.

(2)   Instruction preparation software: BAJI Forms on Disk and CALJIC Forms on Disk.

New and revised instructions are reported in the advance sheets to West's California Reporter (see §5.7.).

Jury instructions are also available in California Forms of Jury Instructions; 1985; Matthew Bender; looseleaf; four volumes; forms available on disk.

§4.24   COURT AND JUDGES DIRECTORIES

There are many directories to federal and state courts and judges. The following are illustrative:

California Courts Directory and Fee Schedule; annual edition; Association of Municipal Court Clerks of California [(916) 345-2752]; softcover; includes court fees for all California courts.

California Courts and Judges Handbook by Arnold (5th edition); 1988; Law Book Service Company; hardcover; one volume; court directories; judicial biographies; tables.

California Legal Filing Directory; 1988; Shepard's; looseleaf; one volume; fees; document requirements; court directory.

Judicial Profiles; Daily Journal Corporation; looseleaf; six volumes; biographical sketches of state and federal judges first appearing in the Los Angeles Daily Journal.

BNA's Directory of State Courts, Judges and Clerks: A State by State Listing (third edition); 1990; Bureau of National Affairs (BNA) [(916) 552-6500].

Almanac of the Federal Judiciary; 1990; Prentice Hall; looseleaf; two volumes; available on Westlaw.

National Directory of Courts of Law; 1991; Information Resources Press [(703) 558-8270]; federal and state judges.

D.C. Federal Courts Handbook; 1988; Prentice Hall; looseleaf; one volume; information, judicial biographies, court rules.

United States Court Directory; 1991; Administrative Office of the United States Courts; looseleaf; one volume.

The American Bench (sixth edition); 1991; Foster-Long (Sacramento); biographical information.

Many legal newspapers publish periodic court directories, often quarterly. The Recorder (see §9.12), for example, publishes a quarterly guide that includes information about state and federal courts in the San Francisco Bay Area. It also includes advertising for legal services. In addition, many lawyer directories include court directories for local state and federal courts. For example, the Directory of San Francisco Attorneys published by the Bar Association of San Francisco includes a directory of courts in the San Francisco Bay Area. (On lawyer directories, see §3.7.)

Each bound volume of the California Official Reports (see §5.4) lists the names of judges of the Supreme Court, the Courts of Appeal and the superior courts.

CHAPTER 5

CASE LAW

This chapter introduces the law produced by the judicial branch, focusing on the reporting and publishing of cases, and the tools available for finding case law.

§5.1	Common Law	68
§5.2	Court Opinions	69
§5.3	Reports and Reporters	69
§5.4	Publication of Opinions in California	71
§5.5	Advance Reports	72
§5.6	Bancroft Whitney Advance Sheets	74
§5.7	West Advance Sheets	76
§5.8	Appellate Department	77
§5.9	Selective Publication	78
§5.10	Depublication	79
§5.11	Time Deadlines in the Appellate Process	80
§5.12	Subsequent History Table	80
§5.13	California Citation Guide	81
§5.14	Federal Cases	82
§5.15	West Reporter System	84
§5.16	Tips for Finding Cases	85
§5.17	Case Briefs	86
§5.18	Digests	87
§5.19	Bancroft Whitney Digests	88
§5.20	West Digests	89
§5.21	West Key Number System	90
§5.22	ALR (American Law Reports)	91
§5.23	Restatements	93

---

§5.1   COMMON LAW

At the core of the American legal system is the concept of the common law, that is, the body of nonstatutory law produced by the judicial branch of government in the form of court opinions. The terms "common law," "case law," and "unwritten law" are synonymous. In resolving disputes between litigants, courts rely not only on written or enacted law (statutes and constitutions) but on rules or principles of law developed over time in the resolution of disputes and the interpretation of statutes by courts.

In some circumstances, reliance on common law is authorized by statute. For example, Probate Code §15002 provides: "Except to the extent that the common law rules governing trusts are modified by statute, the common law as to trusts is the law of this state." (On the Restatement as the expression of common law, see §5.23.) Two concepts support the common law system:

(1)   Precedent. A precedent is an earlier case that furnishes an example or authority for a similar set of facts or a similar question of law.

(2)   Stare Decisis. This Latin expression is roughly equivalent to "Let the decision stand". The basic concept of stare decisis is that established principles of law are not lightly disregarded. When a court has articulated a principle of law applicable to a given set of facts, that court and lower courts will adhere to the principle and apply it in later cases in which the facts are substantially the same.

Reliance on these two concepts leads to the need to report (publish) cases. (On reports, see §5.3.)

The term "common law" is also used to refer to the law of England, which was appropriated by the American states at the time of independence, and which theoretically remains a part of American law until superseded.

§5.2   COURT OPINIONS

In determining disputes between litigants, appellate courts and some trial courts prepare written explanations of the issues involved, the results reached, and the reasoning justifying the results. The equivalent terms "opinions," "decisions," and "cases" describe these writings. Sometimes, these court opinions are published. They are to be distinguished from the transcripts of trial court cases (prepared by court reporters) which are not published. Memorandum decisions are brief appellate decisions that generally state only the result. Ordinarily memorandum opinions are not published, but there are exceptions. For example, federal tax court memorandum decisions are published.

§5.3   REPORTS AND REPORTERS

"Reports" and "reporters" are the generic terms for books in which court opinions are published. If published by the state or by a private publisher under the supervision of the state, or designated by the state, a report or reporter is "official." If privately published without supervision or designation, a report or reporter is "unofficial."

Components of Published Opinion. A published opinion generally consist of the following:

(1) Caption: names of the parties
(2) Identification of the parties and the judge writing the opinion
(3) Summary of the opinion
(4) Headnotes: brief summaries of each point of law set forth in the opinion
(5) Text of the opinion, including:
    (a) Facts of the case to be decided (the context)
    (b) The legal issues or questions the opinion will address (the questions)
    (c) The decision or holding (the result)
    (d) The court's reasoning (the explanation)

(6)   Concurring and dissenting opinions

Contents of Reporter. Generally, a volume of case reports contains (1) the text of opinions (in chronological order of the time of decision), (2) a table of cases appearing in the volume, (3) a table of citations in the reported cases to constitutions, statutes, codes, and rules, (4) a list of judges, and (5) a topical index.

Editorial Content of Opinions. The court opinions themselves are written by judges and are "the law." The summary, headnotes and finding aids are prepared by the editorial staff of the publisher and are not part of the opinion of the judge. They are useful for reference, but may not be cited as legal authority.

Citation. The citation of a case identifies the case and its location in the relevant reports. The citation should provide sufficient information for a legal researcher to find the case. If the case is published in more than one reporter, the unofficial (or parallel) citations is ordinarily given after the official citation. However, California Rules of Court, Rule 313(c), applicable to briefs and memoranda of points and authorities, provides that a case citation must include the official report volume and page number and year of decision; no other citation shall be required.

By convention, the citation includes the case name, the year, the reporter volume number, the reporter abbreviation, and the first page of opinion. Nevertheless, publications and style manuals are not consistent; e.g., recognized abbreviations vary, and dates may appear after the name or after the reporter information.

A point page is a specific page of an opinion after the first page. Once the complete citation has been given, a reference to a point page should identify the volume, reporter, and point page without repetition of the case name and initial page, e.g., 10 Cal. App. 4th at 171.

§5.4 PUBLICATION OF OPINIONS IN CALIFORNIA

California cases are published in both official and unofficial versions. The official reports are published by Bancroft Whitney and consist of the following:

(1) California Reports
Supreme Court cases from 1850 to 1934; volumes 1 to 220
Citation: [volume] Cal. or C. [page]; e.g., 17 Cal. 105.

(2) California Reports, Second Series
Supreme Court cases from 1934 to 1969; volumes 1 to 71
Citation: [volume] Cal. 2d or C. 2d [page]; e.g., 45 Cal. 2d 575.

(3) California Reports, Third Series
Supreme Court cases from 1969 to 1991; volumes 1 to 54
Citation: [volume] Cal. 3d or C. 3d [page]; e.g., 47 Cal. 3d 22.

(4) California Reports, Fourth Series
Supreme Court Cases from 1992 to date; volumes 1+
Citation: [volume] Cal. 4th or C. 4th [page]; e.g., 5 Cal. 4th 107.

(5) California Appellate Reports
Court of Appeal cases from 1905 to 1934; volume 1 to 140.
Citation: [volume] Cal. App. or C.A. [page]; e.g., 45 Cal. App. 92.

(6) California Appellate Reports, Second Series
Court of Appeal cases from 1934 to 1969; volumes 1 to 276.
Citation: [volume] Cal. App. 2d or C.A. 2d [page]; e.g., 243 Cal. App. 2d 704.

(7) California Appellate Reports, Third Series
Court of Appeal cases (and appellate department cases) from 1969 to 1991; volumes 1 to 235
Citation: [volume] Cal. App. 3d or C. A. 3d [page]; e.g., 14 Cal. App. 3d 100.

(8)   California Appellate Reports, Fourth Series
      Court of Appeal cases (and appellate department cases)
      from 1992 to date; volumes 1+
      Citation: [volume] Cal. App. 4th or C. A. 4th [page];
      e.g., 11 Cal. App. 4th 73.

The unofficial reports are published by West and consist of
the following:

(1)   Pacific Reporter
      Supreme Court Cases from 1883 to 1931 and Court of Appeal
      cases from 1905 to 1931; volumes 1-300
      Citation: [volume] P. or Pac. [page]; e.g. 171 P. 507.

(2)   Pacific Reporter, Second Series
      Supreme Court cases from 1931 to date and Court of Appeal
      Cases from 1931 to 1959; volumes 1-700+
      Citation: [volume] P.2d [page]; e.g. 133 P.2d 299.

(3)   California Reporter; cases from the California Supreme
      Court, the Courts of Appeals and the Appellate Department
      of the Superior Court from 1959 to 1991; volumes 1-286.
      Citation: 211 C.R. 100; 211 Cal. Rptr 100.

(4)   California Reporter, Second Series; cases from the
      California Supreme Court, the Courts of Appeal and the
      Appellate Department of the Superior Court from 1991 to
      date; volumes 1+
      Citation: 1 C.R. 2d 100; 1 Cal. Rptr 2d 100

Both official and unofficial reports are available in CD-ROM
format.   (See §12.9.)

§5.5   ADVANCE REPORTS

Slip Opinions. Court opinions are first issued individually,
on the day of decision, in an unannotated format.   These "slip
opinions" are available to the public, newspapers, and publishers.

Electronic Bulletin Board. The opinions of the California appellate courts are available electronically through the Judicial Council's electronic Bulletin Board Service (BBS). The Administrative Office of the Courts (see §4.11) provides communications software to those who register for the service. The service also includes new and amended California Rules of Court, and the Supreme Court's oral argument calendar. (415) 396-9277.

Newspapers. Legal newspapers (see §9.12) frequently publish the full text of court opinions within several days after the date the opinion is issued by the court. Two major legal newspapers in California do so:

(1) Daily Journal. The Daily Appellate Report (D.A.R.), published in conjunction with the newspapers published by the Daily Journal Corporation, publishes the full text of opinions Monday through Friday, generally within a week and frequently within a day or two of the filing date. It reports opinions of the California Supreme Court, the California Courts of Appeal, the California Attorney General, the State Bar Court, the United States Supreme Court, the Ninth Circuit Court of Appeals (including the Ninth Circuit Bankruptcy Appellate Panel), and the United States District Courts in California. A monthly index includes (1) a table of cases and citations, (2) a subject matter index, and (3) a table of decertification orders. A semi-monthly supplement provides a list of pending cases.

Citation: [year] Daily Journal D.A.R. [page]
91 Daily Journal D.A.R. 1000.

(2) Recorder. The California Daily Opinion Service, published in conjunction with The Recorder, publishes summaries and the full text of opinions Monday through Friday, generally within a week and frequently within a day or two of the filing date. It reports opinions of the California Supreme Court, the California Courts of Appeal, the United States Supreme Court, the Ninth Circuit Court of Appeals (including the Ninth Circuit Bankruptcy Appellate Panel), and some opinions of the United States District Courts in California. A monthly index (published on the last Monday of the month)

includes a cumulative list of depublished cases for the year.

Citation: [year] C.D.O.S. [page]
91 C.D.O.S. 1000.

Online Services. California cases are available on line from Lexis, Westlaw, and Attorney's BriefCase (see §12.3 et seq.).

§5.6   BANCROFT WHITNEY ADVANCE SHEETS

The official reports in California are published in two bound sets, California Reports and California Appellate Reports. However, the advance sheets for these two publications comprise a single publication, called California Official Reports, Advance Sheets. The advance sheets consist of soft-covered pamphlets, consecutively numbered throughout the calendar year, issued approximately every ten days.

A single pamphlet usually contains pages that will eventually be issued in two or three bound volumes. The publisher distinguishes these bound volume destinations by color or marking on the pages. The green pages are Supreme Court cases and appear in California Reports bound volumes. The white pages are Court of Appeal (and superior court appellate department) cases and appear in California Appellate Reports bound volumes. Where two bound volumes of the California Appellate Reports are represented in the same advance pamphlet, the earlier volume is indicated by white pages and the later volume is indicated by pages with black and white stripes on the outside margin.

To facilitate correct citation, the advance pamphlet page numbers correspond to the page numbers to be used in the bound volume. This procedure has several consequences:

(1)   If a case once published in the advance sheets is ordered depublished or review or rehearing is granted, the pages in the bound volume are retired. Thus, a page in the bound volume may contain a notice such as: Opinion (Smith v. Jones) on pages 107-133 omitted. A footnote will

explain the reason: e.g., Deleted on direction of Supreme Court by order dated January 22nd, 1991. (On depublication, see §5.10.)

(2) If the opinion is a case is not final when the bound volume is published (generally when review of an opinion of the Court of Appeal is granted by the Supreme Court but the Supreme Court has not yet issued its own opinion), the opinion is reprinted in the advance sheets with a new citation. This allows bound volumes to be published on schedule and out-dated advance pamphlets to be discarded, and preserves pending opinions, but prevents the publication in the bound volume of opinions that may eventually be ordered depublished. The bound volume will contain a notice that the case is omitted and provide an explanatory footnote: Review granted. Reprinted without change in ___ Cal.App.4th ___ to permit tracking pending review by the Supreme Court.

The cover of each pamphlet is dated and includes a list of cases in that pamphlet, with a brief description of the subject matter (continued inside the front and back covers). The spine indicates the year, the pamphlet number, and the pages in the eventual bound volume included in the pamphlet. Periodically, an advance pamphlet includes recently enacted or amended state or local rules or forms. When this is the case, the spine indicates "Rules".

Each pamphlet includes a table of Supreme Court cases, tables of statutes, and indexes, which are cumulative with respect to the bound volume to which they relate. Each pamphlet also includes a table of Court of Appeal cases and a table of official digest classifications which are cumulative for six months. Pamphlets marked with an asterisk on the spine indicate that the final cumulative tables for the preceding six months are in that pamphlet. The virtue of six month cumulation is that named cases can be located by looking in only two or three pamphlets.

The outside margin of each page in the advance pamphlet has a number corresponding to the various parts of the pamphlet, which functions like the tab in a notebook. The numbers indicate the following:

Green Pages.

(1) Supreme Court cases reported in that pamphlet
(2) Summary of cases accepted for review by the Supreme Court
(3) Multivolume cumulative table of Supreme Court cases
(4) Supreme Court opinions
(5) Supreme Court minutes
(6) Citation guide to overruled and disapproved cases (an advance version of material which will appear in the California Citation Guide; see §5.13)
(7) Cumulative table of statutes cited in Supreme Court cases in that bound volume
(8) Recent changes in rules and forms ("Rules" on the spine)

White Pages.

(1) Court of Appeal opinions reported in that pamphlet
(2) Multivolume cumulative table of Court of Appeal and appellate department cases
(3) Court of Appeal opinions
(4) Superior Court appellate department opinions
(5) Multivolume cumulative table of official digest classifications for Supreme Court and Court of Appeal cases
(6) Court of Appeal minutes
(7) Cumulative table of statutes cited in Court of Appeal cases in that bound volume
(8) Multivolume cumulative subsequent history table for Supreme Court and Court of Appeal cases (always use the table in the most recent pamphlet) (see §5.12)
(9) Multivolume table of review granted cases (Alphabetical by name and by citation)
(10) Multivolume table of depublished opinions (Alphabetical by name and by citation)

§5.7   **WEST ADVANCE SHEETS**

The advance sheets for West's California Reporter are softcover pamphlets consecutively numbered and issued every seven days. They contain cased decided in the California Supreme Court, the Courts of Appeal and the appellate department of the superior court. Advance pamphlet page numbers correspond to the page numbers used in the bound volume. Because the California Reporter is unofficial, it is not bound by California's depublication Procedure (see §5.10). This means that depublished cases are included in the bound volume.

Each pamphlet also contains (a) a cumulative table of cases, (b) tables of statutes and rules, (c) a cumulative list of words and phrases defined in the opinions, and (d) a key number digest (a preview of classifications in West's California Digest). In addition, a feature called California Law Weekly includes the following:

(1) A table of recent citations to jury instructions and the text of revised jury instructions (on jury instructions, see §4.23)

(2) Recent law review references, by topic

(3) Recent attorney general opinion references and digests

(4) California Case History Table

(5) California Cumulative Review, Rehearing and Hearing Table

(6) Parallel Citation Table

(7) Survey of recent state and federal opinions

(8) Legislative highlights

§5.8   APPELLATE DEPARTMENT

Cases in the municipal or justice court that are appealed are heard by the appellate department of the superior court (superior court judges functioning as appellate judges). If such an appeal results in a published opinion, it is published in a supplement to the California Appellate Reports. These cases appear at the end of the volume and are cited with the designation "Supp.", e.g.: 212 C.A.3d Supp. 6. Appellate department cases are also published in West's California Reporter.

§5.9   SELECTIVE PUBLICATION

In many states, all appellate opinions are officially published. In California, opinions are officially published only selectively. Nearly 6000 opinions are written annually by the Courts of Appeal, of which approximately 11 percent are published. The California Constitution (Art. VI, §14) authorizes the Legislature to provide for publication of opinions "as the Supreme Court deems appropriate." Under Government Code §68902, the authority to set guidelines for publication is delegated to the Supreme Court. Selective publication is governed by the California Rules of Court as follows:

(1) All Supreme Court opinions are published. (Rule 976.)

(2) Appellate opinions superseded by a grant of review or rehearing are not generally published. (The Supreme Court may order the opinion published in whole or in part.)

(3) Under Rule 976, opinions of the Court of Appeal and the appellate department of the superior court are published if a majority of the panel rendering the decision certifies that the opinion meets one of the following standards:

    (a) Establishes a new rule of law, applies an existing rule to a set of facts substantially different from those stated in published opinions, or modifies or criticizes (with reasons given) an existing rule.

    (b) Resolves or creates an apparent conflict in the law.

    (c) Involves a legal issue of continuing public interest.

    (d) Makes a significant contribution to legal literature by reviewing either the development of a common law rule or the legislative or judicial history of a provision of a constitution, statute, or other written law.

(4) Part of an opinion may be published. The published portion will note in footnotes that a portion of the opinion is not being published. (See Rule 976.1.)

(5) Subject to specified exceptions, unpublished opinions may not be cited or relied on by courts or parties. (Rule 977.)

§5.10   DEPUBLICATION

Because of California's selective publication rules (see §5.9), opinions that actually appear in advance reports and the advance sheets may later be ordered not certified for official publication. This process is called "decertification" or "depublication." Depublished opinions are not included in the bound volume of the official reports (Bancroft Whitney) and are not recognized as authority by California courts. (These decisions may not be cited to the California courts; see §5.9.) The unofficial reports (West; newspapers; online services) are not bound by this publication restriction and often publish superseded or decertified cases. (On depublication generally, see Uelman, Waiting for Thunderclaps, California Lawyer (June, 1993) p. 29.)

Illustration: The opinion of the California Court of Appeal in Isbister v. Boys Club of Santa Cruz, was published in the California Official Reports Advance Sheets at 144 Cal. App. 3d 338 and in the California Reporter Advance Sheets at 192 Cal. Rptr 560. The California Supreme Court granted review and the opinion of the Court of Appeal was thus "depublished." The opinion is not published in the bound volume of California Appellate Reports. At 144 Cal. App. 3d 338 is a notice that the opinion has been omitted from the bound volume. The opinion is published in the bound volume of California Reporter. The opinion of the California Supreme Court in the same case is published in California Reports, California Reporter, and Pacific Reporter.

Cases published in the bound volumes of the official reports are final and may be cited. Because a California Court of Appeal case in an advance report (Lexis; Westlaw; newspapers; official or unofficial advance sheets) or in West's California Reporter bound volumes may be depublished, it should always be verified before it is relied upon. The following sources may be used to determine whether a case has been depublished:

(1)   California Official Reports Advance Sheets; cumulative subsequent history table (tab 8 in the white pages) (See §5.12)
(2)   California Appellate Reports, 3d, table of depublished opinions (see §5.6)
(3)   Recorder; monthly index
(4)   Daily Journal; monthly index
(5)   West's California Reporter; Case History Table
(6)   West's Cumulative Review, Rehearing and Hearing Table (annual; updated in California Reporter advance sheets)
(7)   Shepard's California Citations and California Reporter Citations
(8)   Lexis (autocite); Westlaw (instacite)

§5.11   TIME DEADLINES IN THE APPELLATE PROCESS

A Court of Appeal opinion is final in the Court of Appeal 30 days after filing. A petition for rehearing must be filed within that period. A petition for review in the Supreme Court must be filed within 10 days after the opinion is final in the Court of Appeal. The Supreme Court has 60 days after the petition for review is filed to order review and may extend the time to order review up to an additional 30 days. In the absence of a petition for review, the Supreme Court may order review on its own motion within 30 days after the opinion is final in the Court of Appeal and may extend the time to order review up to an additional 60 days. (See California Rules of Court, Rules 24 and 28.)

§5.12   SUBSEQUENT HISTORY TABLE

The Cumulative Subsequent History Table appears in each pamphlet of the California Official Reports Advance Sheets. It lists California cases alphabetically by name. For each case listed, the table gives the advance sheet citation and provides information from which a researcher can determine the current status and viability of the case. It will reveal, for example, whether a petition for rehearing or review has been filed, granted, or denied, or whether the time to file or determine a petition has been extended. Its use is explained in the preface to the table.

The following list illustrates the kind of subsequent history an opinion published in the advance sheets may have:

(1) A Court of Appeal opinion may be ordered depublished.

(2) The Supreme Court may grant review of a Court of Appeal opinion, thereby superseding the opinion in the Court of Appeal. An opinion for which review has been granted may sometimes be reprinted at another location in the advance sheets for tracking pending review. This allows the superseded Court of Appeal opinion to exist in the advance sheets until the superseding Supreme Court opinion is final.

(3) A Supreme Court or Court of Appeal opinion may be modified. If the modification is substantial, the opinion may be reported at a new location in the advance sheets.

(4) An opinion may be written on denial of a rehearing.

§5.13   CALIFORNIA CITATION GUIDE

Originally a hardcover companion to the California Digest of Official Reports (Bancroft Whitney) (see §5.19), the California Citation Guide also appears in an annual softcover version. It contains (1) a chronological list (by citation) of overruled and disapproved California cases with explanatory notes, (2) a table of cases, by plaintiff and defendant, (3) a parallel citation table of unofficial citations, and (4) a table of depublished cases. Overrulings and disapprovals more recent than the current volume appear in a California Citation Guide Table, published in each pamphlet of the California Official Reports Advance Sheets (tab 8 in the green pages) (see §5.6).

This publication can be an extremely useful tool. A researcher with the name or citation to a California case is able to determine whether the case has been overruled or disapproved and to read a short statement of the points and reasoning involved.

§5.14   FEDERAL CASES

U.S. Supreme Court Cases.

   Reporters:

   (1)   U. S. Reports (1790-date)
         Citation: U.S.
         Publisher: U.S. Government
   (2)   Supreme Court Reporter (1882-date)
         Citation: S.Ct.
         Publisher: West
   (3)   U.S. Supreme Court Reports, Lawyers' Edition
         (1790-1956); second edition (1956-date)
         Citation: L.Ed; L.Ed.2d
         Publisher: LCP

   Digests:

   (1)   Supreme Court Digest
   (2)   Supreme Court Digest, Lawyers' Edition
   (3)   Federal Practice Digest 4th
   (4)   Federal Practice Digest 3d
   (5)   Federal Practice Digest 2d
   (6)   Modern Federal Practice Digest
   (7)   Federal Digest
   (8)   Decennial Digests

U.S. Courts of Appeal Cases.

   Reporters:

   (1)   Federal Reporter 2d (1924-date)
         Citation: F.2d
         Publisher: West

(2) Federal Reporter (1880-1924)
     Citation: F
     Publisher: West
(3) Federal Cases (1789-1880)
     Citation; F. Cas.

Digests:

(1) Federal Practice Digest 4th
(2) Federal Practice Digest 3d
(3) Federal Practice Digest 2d
(4) Modern Federal Practice Digest
(5) Federal Digest
(6) Decennial Digests

U.S. District Court Cases.

Reporters:

(1) Federal Supplement (1932-date)
     Citation: F. Supp.
(2) Federal Reporter and Federal Reporter 2d (1880-1932)
     Citation: F; F.2d
(3) Federal Cases (1789-1880)
     Citation: F. Cas.
(4) Federal Rules Decisions (1938-date)
     Citation: F.R.D.

Digests:

(1) Federal Practice Digest 4th
(2) Federal Practice Digest 3d
(3) Federal Practice Digest 2d
(4) Modern Federal Practice Digest
(5) Federal Digest
(6) Decennial Digests

Specialized Reporters of Federal Cases.

Tax Court Reports
Citation: TC

Board of Tax Appeals
Citation: BTA

United States Tax Cases (Commerce Clearing House)
Citation: USTC

American Federal Tax Reporter (Prentice Hall)
Citation: AFTR

§5.15   WEST REPORTER SYSTEM

West Publishing Company publishes most state and federal cases. It does so in a geographical system called the National Reporter System. Each of its regional reporters includes cases from states in a geographical area. They are:

Atlantic Reporter: Connecticut; Delaware; District of Columbia; Maine, Maryland, New Hampshire; New Jersey; Pennsylvania; Rhode Island, Vermont. Citation: A. (1885-1938); A.2d (1938-date)

North Eastern Reporter: Illinois, Indiana, Massachusetts, New York (Court of Appeals); Ohio. Citation: N.E. (1885-1936); N.E.2d (1936-date)

Northwestern Reporter: Iowa: Michigan: Minnesota; Nebraska: North Dakota; South Dakota; Wisconsin. Citation: N.W. (1879-1942); N.W.2d (1942-date)

Pacific Reporter: Alaska: Arizona; California (Supreme Court); Colorado; Hawaii; Idaho; Kansas; Montana; Nevada; New Mexico; Oklahoma; Oregon; Utah; Washington; Wyoming. Citation: P. (1881-1931); P.2d, (1931-date)

South Eastern Reporter: Georgia; North Carolina; South Carolina; Virginia; West Virginia. Citation: S.E. (1887-1939); S.E.2d (1939-date)

Southern Reporter: Alabama; Florida; Louisiana; Mississippi. Citation: So. (1887-1941); So.2d (1941-date)

South Western Reporter: Arkansas; Kentucky; Missouri; Tennessee; Texas. Citation: S.W. (1886-1928); S.W.2d (1928-date)

New York Supplement: All New York appellate courts

California Reporter: All California appellate courts (see §5.4.)

§5.16 TIPS FOR FINDING CASES

Finding Cases by Name. The following sources are available for finding a case citation if the name of the case is known:

(1) Digests. Each digest generally has an alphabetical case table of cases covered in the digest.

(2) Popular Name Tables. Significant cases are often identified by popular name in popular name tables. Shepard's Federal Acts and Cases by Popular Name is an example. Shepard's California Case Name Citator lists all California cases since 1950 by plaintiff and defendant. (See §11.4.)

(3) California Official Reports. The California Official Reports, 3d series (cases from 1969 to 1991) include a three volume table of cases (buff and red). One volume includes California Supreme Court cases. Two volumes include California Court of Appeal cases (A through O and P through Z). Cases are listed by both plaintiff and defendant in the citation format required by the California Style Manual, and parallel citations are given.

(4) Table of Cases. Treatises and practice works frequently include a table of cases cited. Witkin is an example.

Finding Cases by Topic. The following sources are available for finding cases involving a legal or factual point:

(1) Digests. Digests typically arrange brief summaries of points of law for individual cases. (See §5.18.)

(2) <u>Annotated Codes</u>. Cases interpreting or applying statutes are noted as annotations following each statute. (See §7.6.)

(3) <u>ALR Annotations</u>. Each annotation discusses and cites cases within the scope of the annotation's subject matter. (See §5.22.)

(4) <u>Commentary and Practice Works</u>. These sources provide citations for cases cited or discussed as authority.

§5.17   CASE BRIEFS

A case brief is a concise written summary of a court opinion. It extracts and restates the significant information in the opinion in a format that allows a researcher to recall specific information quickly and compare and contrast the briefed opinion with others. Because a case brief is primarily a mechanism for preserving research, the style and format can be flexible. (Unlike briefs on appeal, a case brief is not a document filed with the court.)

Generally, a case brief should include or identify the following:

(1) Title; citations (official and unofficial); date

(2) Parties (names, status, relation to each other)

(3) Causes of action and defenses; contentions of the parties

(4) The facts (what happened to the parties before the first paper was filed; focus on key facts - those which, if changed, would have an impact on the outcome)

(5) Procedural history (what happened from the time the first paper was filed until the time this opinion was written; what happened at the trial court; how did the case get to this court)

(6) Issue (question to be resolved by this opinion; what is this court being asked to decide)

(7) Holding (answer to the question stating the issue)

(8) Reasoning (explanation by which the court justifies the holding)

(9) Disposition (what the court orders)

Briefs may also include:

(a) Concurring and dissenting opinions (brief explanation)

(b) Results of Shepardizing (see §11.3)

(c) Analysis (relevance and weight; points for further study)

§5.18   DIGESTS

A digest is an index to case law. It provides a way to identify cases by topic or by name. Digests may include the cases of a single court, a state, a region, or cases from many courts with respect to a specific topic. For example:

State digest: California Digest
Regional digest: Pacific Digest
Topical digest: California Construction Law Digest (Shepard's)

In case reporters, cases are set out in full text and are generally arranged chronologically. In a digest, cases are set out in brief editorial summaries and arranged topically. The editorial summaries are almost always the headnotes that precede the published opinions in the reporter and it is common for a reporter to have a sister digest. Official digests cover cases from the official reports, and unofficial digests cover cases from the unofficial reports.

Digests are arranged alphabetically by large titles or chapters, which are in turn divided into sections. In the West system, the sections are called key numbers and tend to be consistent throughout the West system. (On key number system, see §5.21.)

Digests generally provide a topical index, a table of cases, and a words and phrases index. Often, each volume includes an alphabetical list of digest topics and a topical outline of digest topics and subtopics.

§5.19   BANCROFT WHITNEY DIGESTS

The official digest in California has the following elements:

New California Digest (McKinney's); California cases up to 1969; hardcover (blue). Volume 1A - Rules of Court; Volumes 1B-26 - A to Z chapters; Vol 27A-27C - Table of Cases; Volumes 28A-28D - General Index; four additional volumes - California Words, Phrases and Maxims.

California Digest of Official Reports, Third Series; California cases since 1969; hardcover (buff); approximately 26 volumes without volume numbers but in alphabetical order; periodic replacement volumes; annual pocket part supplements and an interim supplement pamphlet; table of cases by plaintiff and defendant (1 volume) and a table of statutes and index (1 volume). Digest classifications more recent than the current supplement appear in a Table of Official Digest Classifications, published in each pamphlet of the California Official Reports Advance Sheets (tab 8 in the white pages) (see §5.6). Each title includes relevant case notes, annotation references, periodical references and collateral references. Each volume includes (1) a list of all titles in the set, (2) a table of McKinney digest titles and corresponding official digest titles, and (3) parallel reference tables (linking McKinney digest classifications and official digest classifications).

Citation: Set title / chapter title / section number.
          California Digest Official Reports, 3d, Adoption
          §5.

Bancroft Whitney also publishes two topical digests:

California Personal Injury Digest; 1991; looseleaf (blue); 2 volumes.

Miller and Starr California Real Estate Digest; 1991; looseleaf (blue); 2 volumes.

§5.20   WEST DIGESTS

The world's largest publisher of case digests is West Publishing Company. It publishes the following, among others:

California Digest; California and federal cases to 1950; 50 volumes; hardcover (maroon), Volumes 1-3 - Descriptive word index; Volumes 4-46 A to Z chapters; Volumes 47-49A - tables of cases (by plaintiff and by defendant); Volume 50 - words and phrases.

California Digest 2d; California and federal cases since 1950; hardcover (green); 53 volumes; pocket parts and semi-annual softcover supplement; Volumes 1-44 and some A volumes - A to Z chapters; Volumes 45-47 - Word Index; Volumes 48-49 - Table of Cases; Volume 50 - Table of cases by defendant; words and phrases.

Citation: Set title / chapter title / key number
         West's California Digest 2d, Courts, key # 47.

Pacific Digest; Pacific Reporter cases
Volumes 1-100; cases to 1941
Volumes 101-366; cases 1941 to 1962
Volumes 367+; cases 1962 to date

Federal Digest; federal cases to 1939
Modern Federal Practice Digest; federal cases 1939 to 1961
Federal Practice Digest 2d; federal cases 1961 to 1975
Federal Practice Digest 3d; federal cases 1975 to 1989
Federal Practice Digest 4th; federal cases from 1989 to date

Century Digest; state and federal cases 1658 to 1896

Decennial Digests: state and federal cases
     First Decennial 1897 to 1906
     Second Decennial 1907 to 1916
     Third Decennial 1916 to 1926
     Fourth Decennial 1926 to 1936
     Fifth Decennial 1936 to 1946
     Sixth Decennial 1946 to 1956
     Seventh Decennial 1956 to 1966
     Eighth Decennial 1966 to 1976
     Ninth Decennial, part 1 1976 to 1981
     Ninth Decennial, part 2 1981 to 1986
     Tenth Decennial, part 1 1986 to 1991
     General Digest, eighth series; state and federal cases
        1991 to date

§5.21   WEST KEY NUMBER SYSTEM

The West key number system is an elaborate system of classifying the law into topics and subtopics. Over the years, West Publishing Company has organized its publications into approximately 450 alphabetical topics which are used in reporters and digests (and on Westlaw) to gather legal authority (mostly case law) on related topics. The alphabetical topics are further subdivided into approximately 90,000 subtopics which are given key numbers. Because each topic begins with key number 1, the proper citation of a key number includes the name of the topic and the number of the subtopic.

The great virtue of the key number system is that it is used throughout West's entire legal research system. For example, Civil Rights, Key # 9.15 is used to locate material on age discrimination in state and federal digests and on Westlaw.

As the law develops and legal terminology changes, some topics become either out-dated or too restrictive. For example, the topic Drunkards has been superseded by the topic Chemical Dependents, and the topic Pawnbrokers and Money Lenders has been superseded by the topic Consumer Credit. Sometimes, part of a topic is moved to another location. For example, Drugs and Narcotics, Key numbers 151 to 158 have been moved to Chemical Dependents. Ordinarily, parallel reference tables are available to trace out-dated citations to their current location.

Key numbers are usually whole numbers, but can also be decimals and fractions. Frequently, key numbers are subdivided. The following key numbers, all from the topic Carriers, are illustrative of various numbering formats: # 200; # 217 1/2; # 253.5; # 287(4); # 307(1.5).

§5.22   ALR (AMERICAN LAW REPORTS)

ALR (American Law Reports), published by Lawyers Cooperative Publishing, began as a selective reporter of significant cases nationwide, each followed by a short annotation discussing the key issue of the published case. Today, ALR still includes leading cases, but the heart of the publication is the annotations, which are exhaustive articles on specific points of law.

ALR is an extremely useful research tool, superior to digests for finding relevant and comprehensible case law. Annotations are generally narrow and factual, reflecting the client-oriented and dispute-resolving focus of case law. Illustrations:

(1)   Intoxication of witness or attorney as contempt of court, 46 ALR4th 707

(2)   Government tort liability for failure to provide police protection to specifically threatened crime victim, 46 ALR4th 238

(3)   Identification of job seeker by race, religion, national origin, sex, or age, in "situation wanted" employment advertising as violation of state civil rights laws, 99 ALR3d 154

ALR has had a number of incarnations over the years, with the format and supplementation changing periodically. Generally, significant changes are indicated by a change in the ALR series number. For example, ALR 5th introduced a number of useful research features: (1) citations to relevant state statutes, (2) West key numbers, (3) computer assisted legal research queries, and (4) tables of cases and statutes cite in each volume. However, a later series is neither a replacement nor a supplement to an earlier series. Today, the ALR system includes the following:

(1) ALR 2d; 1948 to 1965; volumes 1 to 100; supplemented with hardcover Later Case Service volumes (blue) which are in turn supplemented with pocket parts

(2) ALR 3d; 1965 to 1980; volumes 1 to 100; pocket part supplements

(3) ALR 4th; 1980 to 1991; volumes 1 to 90; pocket part supplements

(4) ALR 5th; 1992 to date; volumes 1 to 8 (1992); pocket part supplements

(5) ALR Fed; 1969 to date; volumes 1 to 110 (1992); pocket part supplements

(6) L Ed 2d; 1956 to date; volumes 1 to 110 (1992); pocket part supplements

Two elements of ALR are now outdated: ALR (first series) and L Ed (lawyers edition).

Citation: title / volume / publication / page
          Gesture as punishable obscenity, 99 ALR3d 762.

ALR has a six volume index (1992), supplemented with annual pocket part supplements inserted in the front of the volume. It is a comprehensive index to the annotations in ALR2d, ALR3d, ALR4th, ALR5th, ALR Fed and LEd2d. It replaces a similar 1986 index and the former "quick" indexes available with various elements of the ALR system. It is a descriptive word index embracing both legal and factual terms and concepts, with extensive internal cross-refs. Uniform acts are indexed by name.

Tables of cases, statutes, etc. in volume 6 show where cases, statutes, regulations, court rules, uniform and model acts,

Restatements and professional codes of ethics are cited in various annotations.

The Annotation History Table in Volume 6 lists annotations (including those in ALR first and LEd) that have been superseded or supplemented by later annotations. It is useful for verifying citations to older annotations.

Annotations can be Shepardized (see §11.3) and verified through the autocite system on Lexis (see §12.5).

The publisher provides assistance to subscribers in using the index [(800) 527-0403] and about cases issued after publication of supplements [(800) 225-7488].

§5.23   RESTATEMENTS

The Restatements of the Law are an extremely useful but often overlooked research tool. They are the product of the American Law Institute, which was organized in 1923 by a group of legal scholars. Its goal is to present an orderly statement of the general common law of the United States, that is, to restate common law in an authoritative "black letter" format. (On common law, see §5.1.) While not primary authority, the Restatements are frequently cited and highly persuasive, especially in areas where the law of the state is silent. However, the Restatements do not reflect jurisdictional differences and states are free to reject the Restatement view.

From the 1920s to the 1940s, the Institute published Restatements in the following areas:

    (1)   Agency
    (2)   Conflict of Laws
    (3)   Contracts
    (4)   Foreign Relations Law of the United States
    (5)   Judgments
    (6)   Property
    (7)   Restitution
    (8)   Security

(9)   Torts
(10) Trusts

These original Restatements (now commonly known as the first Restatement) were largely revised, rearranged and republished as the Restatement, Second, beginning in the 1950s. Some elements of the third Restatement have also been published.

Each element of the Restatement consists of two parts:

(1)   Text volumes, which contain (a) a detailed outline of chapters and sections, arranged by topic, (b) the official text of the Restatement sections (in boldface), (c) comments, illustrations, and reporter's notes for each section, (d) table of cases, (e) table of statutes, (f) parallel reference table (linking either First and Second Restatement section numbers or tentative draft numbers and official text numbers), and (g) index.

(2)   Appendix volumes, which contain (a) notes of court opinions citing the Restatement, and (b) cross-references to ALR annotations and West key numbers.

The current restatement consists of the following:

(1)   Agency 2d - 2 text and 4 appendix volumes.
(2)   Conflict of Laws 2d - 2 text and 3 appendix volumes.
(3)   Contracts 2d - 3 text and 5 appendix volumes.
(4)   Foreign Relations of the United States 3d - 2 text volumes, softcover pamphlet. There is no second restatement.
(5)   Judgments 2d - 2 text and 2 appendix volumes.
(6)   Property - still in revision; currently includes:
      (a) Property (1st) - 5 text volumes (one superseded).
      (b) Property 2d (Landlord and Tenant) - 2 text volumes.
      (c) Property 2d (Donative Transfers) - 4 text volumes.
(7)   Restitution (1st) - 1 text and 2 appendix volumes.
(8)   Security (1st) - 1 text volume.
(9)   Torts 2d - 4 text and 17 appendix volumes. A Restatement of Products Liability is in the works.
(10) Trusts 2d - 2 text and 3 appendix volumes.

Many libraries also retain text and appendix volumes for earlier Restatements, the Restatement in the Courts Permanent Edition (1932-1944) and Bound Supplements (1944 to 1976). The case citations in these volumes are now included in the various appendix volumes.

The format, numbering and supplementation of the Restatement volumes have changed over the years. Restatement (1st) volumes are dark brown, Restatement, Second, volumes are light brown, and Restatement, Third, volumes are blue. Generally, text volumes and older appendix volumes are not supplemented, while newer appendix volumes are supplemented with annual pocket part supplements, called Restatement in the Courts. The second page of each pocket part lists the volumes and supplements that constitute the complete library for that Restatement. The set includes an additional annual softcover pamphlet supplement - Interim Case Citations to the Restatement of the Law.

> Citation: Restatement, Second, Contracts §131
> Restatement (Second) of Contracts §131
> Restatement, Second, Property (Donative Transfers) §25.

Restatement sections may be Shepardized in Shepard's Restatement of the Law Citations, 1986; one volume; citations in cases beginning in 1975.

To find material in the Restatement, both the detailed outline of sections and the topical index may be used. To find case law following the Restatement, the appendix volumes and Shepard's may be used.

CHAPTER 6

THE LEGISLATIVE BRANCH

This chapter introduces the legislature, the legislative process, and the concept of legislative history.

§6.1	In General	98
§6.2	Federal Legislative System	98
§6.3	California Legislative System	98
§6.4	The Lifecycle of Legislation	99
§6.5	California Assembly Standing Committees	100
§6.6	California Senate Standing Committees	101
§6.7	Statutory Numbering	102
§6.8	Bill Numbering	102
§6.9	Enactment Numbering	103
§6.10	Federal Session Laws	103
§6.11	California Session Laws	104
§6.12	Advance Legislative Services	105
§6.13	Legislative History	106
§6.14	Legislative History Services	107
§6.15	California Legislative Sources	107
§6.16	Federal Legislative Sources	108
§6.17	CCH Congressional Index	109
§6.18	U.S. Code Congressional and Administrative News (USCCAN)	110
§6.19	Congressional Information Service (CIS)	111
§6.20	Pending Legislation	112

---

§6.1   IN GENERAL

The legislative branch produces statutory law. Chronological arrangements of statutory law are called session laws (see §§6.10, 6.11), while subject matter arrangements are called codes, statutes, or revised statutes (see §7.3).

§6.2   FEDERAL LEGISLATIVE SYSTEM

The federal legislature is composed of two houses, the Senate and the House of Representatives. The Senate has one hundred senators, two elected at large from each state, who serve for six year terms. The House has 435 representatives, elected from districts, who serve for two year terms. Both houses have large staffs. A wealth of information about Congress is available. One example is: A Research Guide to Congress: How to Make Congress Work for You (2nd edition); 1991; Legi-Slate [(800) 733-1131].

§6.3   CALIFORNIA LEGISLATIVE SYSTEM

The California legislature is composed of two houses, the Senate and the Assembly. (See generally Cal. Const., Art IV; Government Code §8900 et seq.) (For legislative guides and directories, see §8.2.)

Senate. The Senate has 40 members who serve four year terms. The Lieutenant Governor is the President of the Senate and has a tie-breaking vote. The President Pro Tempore is elected from the membership and is the chairperson of the Senate Rules Committee. The Senate Rules Committee appoints officers and members of Senate committees and assigns bills to committees. It also approves Senate expenditures.

Assembly. The Assembly has 80 members who serve two year terms. The Speaker of the Assembly is elected by the membership. He is the presiding officer and an ex officio member of all

Assembly committees and joint committees. He appoints the officers and members of Assembly committees (except the Rules Committee) and selects Assembly appointees to non-legislative boards and commissions, e.g., the Judicial Council. The Rules committee is composed of an equal number of members nominated by the majority and minority caucuses. The chairperson is appointed by the Speaker. The Rules Committee establishes Assembly rules, supervises and selects the Assembly staff and refers bills to various Assembly committees.

Legislative Staff. The staff of the legislature includes the following:

(1) Legislative Counsel - the Legislature's legal advisor, who prepares a digest of each bill and advises the Legislature of the constitutionality and effect of proposed legislation.

(2) Legislative Analyst - Evaluates the fiscal impact of legislation.

(3) Auditor General - Examines and reports on fiscal proposals from the executive branch.

(4) Committee staff - Each committee of the legislature has a paid staff, which prepares committee reports and documents, material for hearings, and so forth.

§6.4   THE LIFECYCLE OF LEGISLATION

The main business of the legislature, both state and federal, is conducted by committee. The members of each house serve on various committees and subcommittees which have authority over designated topics, e.g., the House Armed Services Committee, Senate Judiciary Committee.

A proposed law (called a bill) is introduced by a member of the legislature and assigned to the committee or committees with authority over the subject matter of the bill. Committees generally hold hearings, receive reports and documents from others, and issue reports. Ordinarily, a committee either (1) recommends that the bill as introduced be enacted by the full house, (2) amends the bill and recommends that the amended version be enacted by the full house, or (3) decides not to send the bill to the full house (the bill is tabled or dies in committee).

Once a bill is recommended by each committee to which it has been assigned, it may be voted on by the entire house, with or without amendments added from the floor. A bill approved by one house then goes to the other house and follows the same committee and amendment procedure. If both houses approve identical language, the bill goes to the chief executive. If the versions of the bill approved by each house are not identical, the bill is sent to a conference committee (members from both houses) to resolve difference and then returned to both houses for approval of identical language. The chief executive may (1) sign the bill into law, (2) do nothing, in which case the bill usually becomes law after a requisite lapse of time, or (3) veto the bill (disapprove and return to both houses). To override a veto, both houses must then approve the bill by a two-thirds vote.

§6.5   CALIFORNIA ASSEMBLY STANDING COMMITTEES

Agriculture
Banking, Finance and Bonded Indebtedness
Education
Elections, Reapportionment and Constitutional Amendments
Environmental Safety and Toxic Materials
Governmental Efficiency, Consumer Protection and New
    Technologies
Governmental Organization
Health
Higher Education
Housing and Community Development
Human Services
Insurance
Judiciary
Labor and Employment
Local Government
Natural Resources

Public Employees, Retirement and Social Security
Public Safety
Revenue and Taxation
Rules
Televising the Assembly
Transportation
Utilities and Commerce
Water, Parks and Wildlife
Ways and Means

§6.6 CALIFORNIA SENATE STANDING COMMITTEES

Agriculture and Water Resources
Appropriations
Banking And Commerce
Bonded Indebtedness and Methods of Financing
Budget and Fiscal Review
Business and Professions
Constitutional Amendments
Education
Elections and Reapportionment
Energy and Public Utilities
Governmental Organization
Health and Human Services
Housing and Urban Affairs
Industrial Relations
Insurance, Claims and Corporations
Judiciary
Local Government
Natural Resources and Wildlife
Public Employment and Retirement
Revenue and Taxation
Rules
Toxic and Public Safety Management
Transportation
Veterans Affairs

§6.7 STATUTORY NUMBERING

Finding legislative material can be confusing for uninitiated researchers because of convoluted numbering systems. Statutory material generally has different numbering systems for three phases of the legislative lifecycle.

(1) While legislation is pending, i.e., in the legislative process, it is referred to by bill number. (On bill numbering, see §6.8.)

(2) At the time of enactment, legislation is officially numbered in a chronological arrangement, and published in the session laws as an official record of legislative business. (On enactment numbering, see §6.9; on session laws, see §§6.10, 6.11.)

(3) Following enactment, legislation is arranged by topic and numbered to reflect that arrangement. (On code numbering, see §7.10.)

§6.8 BILL NUMBERING

In each session of the legislature, bills are numbered in each house in chronological order by date of submission. Thus,

    S 1 = first bill introduced in the U.S. Senate
    HR 1 = first bill introduced in the House of Representatives

    SB 1 = first bill introduced in the California Senate
    AB 1 = first bill introduced in the California Assembly

Bill numbers last for the current Legislature only; there is no connection, for example, between HR 43 in the 99th Congress and HR 43 in the 100th Congress. A bill that is pending when the session ends dies with that session. It may be resurrected in a later Legislature, but it will have a new bill number, reflecting its order of introduction in the new session.

§6.9   ENACTMENT NUMBERING

Once a bill is enacted into law, it is numbered and published in chronological order by date of enactment. The generic name for this official record of legislative business is "session laws" which are published for each session of the legislature. The proper citation for these enactments consists of two parts, the number of the enactment, and the citation of the location in the session laws where the enactment is located. (On session laws, see §§6.10, 6.11.)

§6.10   FEDERAL SESSION LAWS

Federal enactments are generally called public laws. They are compiled chronologically in the federal session laws, called the Statutes at Large. Public laws have a two part numbering system, reflecting the numerical identity of the enacting Congress and the order of enactment. Thus, Public Law number 101-336 is the 336th enactment of the 101st Congress. The law's location in the Statutes at Large is cited by volume and page. Public laws are further subdivided into sections.

> Citation: Public Law designation / Congress / number of
>   enactment / volume / publication / page
>   P.L.# 101-336, 104 Stat 327.

From 1963 to 1974, the Statutes at Large included a Guide to Legislative History of Bills Enacted into Public Law, which provided bill numbers, citations to reports, and references to treatment in the Congressional Record. Beginning in 1974, legislative history references are provided following each public law. Bill numbers have been provided by Statutes at Large since 1903.

§6.11   CALIFORNIA SESSION LAWS

When passed by both houses of the California Legislature, signed by the Governor, and filed with the Secretary of State, a bill becomes enacted into law. It is called a chapter and given a chapter number by the Secretary of State. Chapters are numbered in the chronological order of enactment during the session of the Legislature.   There is a regular session of the Legislature for each calendar year and there may be extraordinary sessions as well. Chapters are available individually from the Legislative Bill Room (see §6.15).

The chapter laws are compiled and published in the session laws, officially known as Statutes and Amendments to the Codes. Chapters are identified by the year of enactment and by chapter number.   The citation may also include the page number of the session laws. Chapter laws are further subdivided into sections.

> Citation: Publication / year/ chapter number / section
> number/ page
> Stats. 1990, chap. 792, §3, p. 1145.

The volumes of the session laws are large and hardcover (buff with black and red trim), and are published annually by the State of California.   The publication contains the California Constitution (as amended), general laws, amendments to the codes, constitutional amendments, and resolutions of the Legislature. Until about 1950, each year consists of a single volume.   Since that time, the number of volumes annually has ranged from two to six. Typically, an annual edition contains the following:

(1)   Note concerning effective dates (includes dates of regular and extraordinary sessions)
(2)   California Constitution and index
(3)   List of officers
(4)   Tables of laws and resolutions adopted
(5)   Text of statutes, code amendments, resolutions, and constitutional amendments
(6)   Legislative Counsel's digest of statutes and resolutions (in a separate volume called "Summary Digest")
(7)   Table of bill numbers, including vetoed bills and corresponding chapter numbers

(8) Messages of the governor (called "Digest Chapters Superior Numbers")

(9) Index

Statutory Record. Periodically, the session laws contain what is called the statutory record, listing code sections and uncodified statutes (general laws) and the year and chapter of treatment (addition, amendment, revision, supplement, and repeal). This is generally published as separate volumes, which exist for the following years: 1850-1932; 1933-1948; 1949-1958; 1959-1968; 1969-1978; 1979-1988.

There is a considerable lag (often several years) between the end of the legislative session and the publication of the session laws. In the interim, advance legislative services (see §6.12) may be used to determine the text of numbered chapters.

§6.12   ADVANCE LEGISLATIVE SERVICES

An advance legislative service publishes session laws for the current session of the legislature and provide an advance version of the following year's supplement to the codes. They should be distinguished from mid-year pamphlets which are essentially supplements to the supplement to an annotated or unannotated code. Annotated codes tend to be supplemented (and unannotated codes tend to be published) early in the year and include legislation effective on January 1st of the current year. The advance legislative service tells what the Legislature is doing in the current year and reports legislative changes that are not ordinarily effective until January 1st of the following year. Two commercial publishers provide advance legislative services for California.

Advance Legislative Service to Deering's California Codes; annual edition; Bancroft Whitney; softcover; 6 to 9 pamphlets issued throughout the year; color changes each year. The set includes:

(1) Text of chapters and legislative counsel's digest
(2) Cumulative index - arranged by topic, with topics arranged alphabetically

    (3)   List of state officials
    (4)   Local court rules
    (5)   Ballot measures
    (6)   Tables - sections added, amended or repealed; bill numbers

California Legislative Service; annual edition; West; softcover; 10 to 13 pamphlets issued throughout the year; color changes each year. The set includes:

    (1)   Text of chapters and legislative counsel's digest
    (2)   Cumulative index - arranged alphabetically
    (3)   List of state officials, Supreme Court judges, Senate and Assembly members and standing committees
    (4)   Changes in court rules in an appendix
    (5)   Ballot measures
    (6)   Tables - sections added, amended or repealed; bill numbers; court rules

§6.13   LEGISLATIVE HISTORY

The topic of legislative history is vast and complex. Very simply, it is the process of examining legislative documents to shed light on the meaning or intent of legislation. For example, a court called upon to apply or construe the term "person" in a statute may look in the legislative record for evidence that the legislature intended the term to include corporations as well as natural persons.

The process of preparing a legislative history has two elements: (1) compiling a list of the documentary sources that might reveal legislative purpose or intent (bibliographic element), and (2) collecting and reviewing the documents (documentary element).

Legislative histories may be compiled and published, e.g., in law reviews, by government agencies, or by commercial publishers. For example, the Legislative History of the Securities Act of 1933 and the Securities Exchange Act of 1934 is available on microform from Rothman; the legislative history of the National Labor

Relations Act, published by the National Labor Relations Board, is available on microfiche from LLMC. The best directory to compiled legislative histories is Sources of Compiled Legislative Histories by Johnson; looseleaf; Rothman.

Three publications are especially useful in preparing a federal legislative history: (1) CCH Congressional Index (see §6.17), (2) U.S. Code Congressional and Administrative News (see §6.18), and Congressional Information Service (see §6.19.)

§6.14   LEGISLATIVE HISTORY SERVICES

A number of professional services provide legislative history for a fee. The following are illustrative:

GAO Legislative History Service; provides access to legislative histories compiled by the General Accounting Office; available from Information on Demand [(800) 999-4463]

Legislative Intent Service; provides extensive legislative history for California statutes and regulations; [(800) 666-1917].

Legitech [(916) 447-1886]. Legitech bill summaries are published in the Daily Journal Sacramento Digest (see §9.12). Legi-Fax provides information on pending California bills via fax (for a fee) [(800) 854-5545]. The Legitech database ia available on line in some public libraries (e.g. Oakland).

§6.15   CALIFORNIA LEGISLATIVE SOURCES

Copies of bills and chapters, as well as some legislative publications and a biennial guide entitled California Legislative Handbook, are available from the Legislative Bill Room, State Capitol, Room B32, Sacramento, CA 95814. The text of current bills and a bill tracking database are available online in each legislator's office. Either print versions or printouts can often be ordered over the phone.

The Senate and the Assembly each publish a file (legislative agenda); journal (official record of legislative business); and history (action taken on all bills, constitutional amendments and resolutions). These are published daily or weekly while the Legislature is in session and cumulated and the end of the session.

Legislative committees can be an invaluable source of useful information, publishing dozens of publications annually. These are often softcover and reasonably priced (or free). New state reports and publications are listed in the weekly Sacramento Digest included in the Los Angeles and Sacramento editions of the Daily Journal.

Illustration: The 1992 Revenue and Taxation Reference Book, published by the California Assembly Revenue and Taxation Committee and for sale from the Assembly Publications Office in Sacramento, provides an overview of California's tax system, a detailed explanation of particular taxes, a glossary of tax terminology, and a list of publications of the Revenue and Taxation Committee.

§6.16   FEDERAL LEGISLATIVE SOURCES

Committee Prints. Studies prepared for Congressional committees are called committee prints. Recent committee prints are often available at government depository libraries.

Congressional Record. Each issue of the Congressional Record includes a Daily Digest, which summarizes Congressional activities. The digest is cumulated annually in a table of public laws called History of Bills Enacted into Public Law.

Digest of Public General Bills and Resolutions. Published by the Congressional Research Service of the Library of Congress since 1936. Includes a summary of public bills and resolutions introduced and public laws enacted and a table of public laws and corresponding bill numbers. The status table covers all bills reported from committees. Indexed by subject matter, author,

popular name, and companion bill numbers. Five cumulative issues during each session of Congress.

Monthly Catalog of United States Government Publications. The Monthly Catalog indexes executive and legislative publications, including committee hearings, committee prints, and Senate and House Reports and Documents, by subject, title, author, and document number.

§6.17   CCH CONGRESSIONAL INDEX

The Congressional Index, published by Commerce Clearing House, has the following features:

(1)   Looseleaf service with weekly updates; used primarily for pending legislation; two volumes

(2)   Main and supplemental subject indexes and author index identify bill numbers

(3)   Features called "House Bills" and "Senate Bills" briefly summarize the content of introduced bills and identify committee assignments

(4)   Features called "Current Status of House Bills" and "Current Status of Senate Bills" identify status of bills for which committee hearings have been held or committee reports issued

(5)   Enacted bills indexed and listed; table of companion bills

(6)   Information about presidential vetoes, voting records; members' biographies; committee assignments

(7)   Newsletter: This Week in Congress

Other CCH services:

(1) CCH Electronic Legislative Search System; online service providing action sheet on each bill and its current status

(2) CCH Legislative Reporting Service; action sheet and full text of bills, amendments and reports on topics selected by subscribers

§6.18 **U.S. CODE CONGRESSIONAL AND ADMINISTRATIVE NEWS (USCCAN)**

U.S. Code Congressional and Administrative News, published by West, is available in many law libraries and has the following features:

(1) Issued monthly in softcover; reissued annually in hardcover volumes for each session of Congress

(2) Statutes and legislative history are published in separate volumes; arranged by public law number; cross-referenced to each other

(3) Statutes volume reproduces the session laws and provides Statutes at Large page numbers

(4) Legislative history volume cites reports and floor debates and selectively publishes the text of committee reports

(5) Topical index and various tables for each edition; USCA includes pinpointed page references to legislative history volumes

(6) Presidential messages to Congress reproduced in softcover issues only

§6.19   CONGRESSIONAL INFORMATION SERVICE (CIS)

Since 1970, the Congressional Information Service has been the unparalleled source for legislative history. Its major publication has the following features:

(1)   Monthly softcover index (called CIS Index to Publications of the U.S. Congress) cumulated quarterly and reissued annually (called CIS Annual) in hardcover

(2)   Part 1 abstracts hearings, reports, prints, and documents; does not provide record of floor debates; Part 2 indexes topics, authors, witnesses, popular names, bills, committee members, report and document numbers; does not cover bills not yet in committee

(3)   Multi-year index generally published every four years, e.g., cumulative index 1987-1990

(4)   Annual volume contains complete bibliographic information for each public law enacted during the session and refers to CIS abstracts - bill number, committee reports, hearings, prints, documents, citations to Congressional Record, related bills; since 1984, separate volume is called Annual Legislative History of U.S. Public Laws

(5)   Relevant documents published after the annual cumulation appear in a revised legislative history in the annual for the next year

(6)   CIS Microfiche Library provides full text of documents abstracted in the CIS Index

Other CIS indexes cover documents before 1970:

    CIS U.S. Congressional Committee Hearings Index
    CIS U.S. Congressional Committee Prints Index
    CIS U.S. Serial Set Index (reports and documents)

§6.20   PENDING LEGISLATION

Many of the same publications and techniques used for legislative history are available to determine the status of pending legislation. To find pending legislation, determine the bill number or the topic of the bill. Check the most recent daily or weekly journal of the appropriate house to determine the status of the bill. Get a copy of the bill from the library, a member of the legislature, or from a legislative committee. In California, contact the Legislative Bill Room (see §6.15). Check a bill tracking file in Lexis or Westlaw.

CHAPTER 7

CONSTITUTIONAL AND STATUTORY LAW

This chapter introduces the arrangement, numbering, and publication of constitutions and statutes, advance legislative services, and uniform laws.

§7.1	Constitutional Law	114
§7.2	California Constitution	114
§7.3	Codification	115
§7.4	United States Code	116
§7.5	California Codes	117
§7.6	Annotated Codes	118
§7.7	Unannotated Codes	120
§7.8	Statutes in Electronic Form	121
§7.9	Statutory Indexes	122
§7.10	Code Numbering	123
§7.11	Prior Law and Former Section	125
§7.12	Effective Date of California Legislation	125
§7.13	Popular Name Tables	126
§7.14	Tips for Finding Statutes	126
§7.15	Numbering of Propositions	127
§7.16	Uniform Laws	128
§7.17	Uniform Acts Adopted in California	129

---

§7.1 CONSTITUTIONAL LAW

Technically speaking, constitutions are not statutory law. They are the product of the people, through constitutional conventions or direct elections, rather than the legislature. Generally, constitutions set forth (1) the structure and powers of the various branches of government, and (2) the fundamental rights of the people. As a practical matter, however, constitutions are treated like statutes in legal research materials, and are arranged, discussed, annotated, indexed, and tabled like statutes.

The United States Constitution is widely available. Both USCS and USCA include annotated versions (see §7.4). An unannotated version is available in the Am.Jur. Deskbook.

§7.2 CALIFORNIA CONSTITUTION

The California Constitution is an element of both Deering's and West's annotated California codes (see §7.5). These annotated versions include (1) the text of the constitution, (2) notes and historical material, (3) case and collateral annotations, and (4) an index. The Constitution is cited by article number and section number, e.g., Cal. Const., Art I, §1. It consists of the following articles:

Article I   Declaration of Rights
Article II   Voting, Initiative and Referendum, and Recall
Article III   State of California
Article IV   Legislative
Article V   Executive
Article VI   Judicial
Article VII   Public Officers and Employees
Article IX   Education
Article X   Water
Article X A   Water Resources Development
Article X B   Marine Resources Protection
Article XI   Local Government
Article XII   Public Utilities
Article XIII   Taxation

Article XIII A [Tax Limitation Initiative - Proposition 13]
Article XIII B Government Spending Limitation
Article IV   Labor Relations
Article XV   Usury
Article XVI   Public Finance
Article XVIII   Amending and Revising the Constitution
Article XIX   Motor Vehicle Revenues
Article XX   Miscellaneous Subjects
Article XXI   Reapportionment
Article XXXIV   Public Housing Project Law

§7.3   CODIFICATION

A chronological arrangement of legislation (session laws; see §§6.10, 6.11) may be sufficient for an official record of legislative business, but a subject matter arrangement is essential for most research questions. Thus, the statutes of all states are arranged or compiled by topic. In most states, a single numbered sequence is used. California and the federal system, in contrast, use a system of separate codes, each with its own numbering system. (On the federal code, see §7.4; on the California codes, see §7.5.)

In California, not all enacted legislation becomes codified. Though uncodified measures are still the law, they may be difficult to find and are often overlooked. Uncodified measures usually appear at the beginning or end of an enacted chapter and can be discovered in the session laws (see §6.11) or the advance legislative services (see §6.12). Occasionally they are reproduced as notes in the annotated codes (see §7.6).

Chapter laws in California are divided into sections, each of which may do one of the following:

(1) Add a new section to the codes
(2) Amend an existing section of the codes
(3) Repeal an existing section of the codes
(4) Enact an uncodified statute
(5) Amend an uncodified statute
(6) Repeal an uncodified statute
(7) State legislative intent

(8) State an urgency condition
(9) State a contingency
(10) Make an appropriation

§7.4   UNITED STATES CODE

The subject matter arrangement of the federal statutes is the United States Code, which is published in an official version (USC) and two commercial versions, United States Code Service (USCS) and United States Code Annotated (USCA). A federal statute is cited by title number and section number, e.g., 26 USC §501. USC includes the following titles:

1	General Provisions
2	The Congress
3	The President
4	Flag and Seal, Seat of Government and the States
5	Government Organization and Employees
6	[reserved]
7	Agriculture
8	Aliens and Nationality
9	Arbitration
10	Armed Forces
11	Bankruptcy
12	Banks and Banking
13	Census
14	Coast Guard
15	Commerce and Trade
16	Conservation
17	Copyrights
18	Crimes and Criminal Procedure
19	Customs Duties
20	Education
21	Food and Drugs
22	Foreign Relations and Intercourse
23	Highways
24	Hospitals and Asylums
25	Indians
26	Internal Revenue Code
27	Intoxicating Liquors

28 Judiciary and Judicial Procedure
29 Labor
30 Mineral Lands and Mining
31 Money and Finance
32 National Guard
33 Navigation and Navigable Waters
34 [reserved]
35 Patents
36 Patriotic Societies and Observances
37 Pay and Allowances of the Uniformed Services
38 Veterans' Benefits
39 Postal Service
40 Public Buildings, Property, and Works
41 Public Contracts
42 The Public Health and Welfare
43 Public Lands
44 Public Printing and Documents
45 Railroads
46 Shipping
47 Telegraphs, Telephones, and Radio Telegraphs
48 Territories and Insular Possessions
49 Transportation
50 War and National Defense; Appendix

§7.5 CALIFORNIA CODES

California's statutes were first codified in 1872, in the Civil Code, the Code of Civil Procedure, the Penal Code, and the Political Code. These codes, and later general laws, sufficed until the Code Commission, formed to revise our statutory law, recommended elimination of the Political Code and the enactment of a variety of additional codes. Today, there are 29 separate codes:

Business and Professions Code
Civil Code
Code of Civil Procedure
Corporations Code
Education Code
Elections Code
Evidence Code

Family Code (to take effect January 1, 1994)
Financial Code
Fish and Game Code
Food And Agriculture Code
Government Code
Harbors and Navigation Code
Health and Safety Code
Insurance Code
Labor Code
Military and Veterans Code
Penal Code
Probate Code
Public Contracts Code
Public Resources Code
Public Utilities Code
Revenue and Taxation Code
Streets and Highways Code
Unemployment Insurance Code
Uniform Commercial Code
Vehicle Code
Water Code (with uncodified water acts)
Welfare and Institutions Code

§7.6   ANNOTATED CODES

Two annotated editions of the California codes are widely used:

Deering's California Codes Annotated; Bancroft Whitney; hardcover (maroon); approximately 170 volumes (selectively replaced); not consecutively numbered; supplemented by annual pocket parts and one mid-year pamphlet (supplement to the supplement); one volume general index issued annually.

West's Annotated California Codes; hardcover (blue); approximately 200 volumes (selectively replaced); consecutively numbered 1-75 with many A and B volumes; supplemented by annual pocket parts and two mid-year pamphlets (supplement to the supplement); each volume includes a list of abbreviations; softcover general index (8 volumes) issued annually.

Deering's and West have the following common features:

(1) Outline. Each code begins with a condensed or detailed outline (also called scheme or analysis) listing the divisions, parts, chapters, articles, and sometimes the sections of the code.

(2) Text of Statutes. The text is the exact wording of the statute as enacted by the Legislature. Section headings are usually written by the publisher and are not part of the statute itself, but the section number is provided by the Legislature.

(3) History Line. The history line gives citations to the session laws that enacted and amended the statute and sometimes includes the original bill numbers.

(4) Editorial Notes. These indicate unusual effective or operative dates (see §7.12) and numbering problems (see §7.10).

(5) Comments. Comments of the Law Revision Commission (see §4.13) and legislative committees.

(6) Annotations. The annotations are headnotes from the publisher's case reporters classified and arranged following the statutory sections to which they refer. If numerous, the annotations for a single section might have a table of contents.

(7) Amendment Notes. These indicate the wording of each change, making it possible to determine the text of a section at a given time. However, when a section is repealed, the commercial publishers tend to discard amendment notes from the supplements and replacement volumes. The information remains available in the session laws.

(8) Forms. Sample forms for various proceedings and transaction authorized by statute.

(9) Index. There is a separate index for each code and a general index.

(10) <u>Constitution and Rules</u>.   The set includes an annotated California Constitution and annotated court rules.

There are some differences in terminology between the two publications: (1) West uses Commercial Code; Deering's uses Uniform Commercial Code; (2) West uses Water Code Appendix; Deering's uses Water Uncodified Acts; (3) West uses Civil and Criminal Rules; Deering's Uses California Rules of Court.

§7.7   UNANNOTATED CODES

Many publishers produce selected elements of the California codes in unannotated or selectively annotated versions. They are useful for a quick look at the current text of the statutes and are generally replaced annually. Usually, unannotated codes include (1) an analysis of the code, (2) a table of sections affected in the previous year, and (3) an index.   Sometimes, selected provisions of the California Code of Regulations (see §8.13) are also included.   The main unannotated codes are the following:

Deering's California Unannotated Practice Codes; annual edition; Bancroft Whitney; softcover or hardcover; three volumes; Volume 1 - Civil Code, Probate Code; Volume 2 - Code of Civil Procedure, Evidence Code, Rules of Court; Volume 3 - Penal Code (includes selected penal provisions of other codes - e.g., Health and Safety Code, Vehicle Code, Welfare and Institutions Code).

Bernhardt's California Real Estate Laws; annual; Bancroft Whitney; softcover; one volume.

The Standard California Codes; annual edition; Matthew Bender; hardcover; one volume; contains the Civil Code, Code of Civil Procedure, Evidence Code, Probate Code, Rules of Court, and selected fee provisions of the Government Code; combined index.

West publishes the following unannotated California codes in annual softcover editions under the general name West's California Codes, Compact Edition: (1) Civil, (2) Civil

Procedure, (3) Commercial, (4) Corporations, (5) Evidence, (6) Penal, (6) Probate.

Parker publishes the following unannotated California codes in annual softcover editions: (1) Business and Professions Code (two volumes), (2) Civil Code, (3) Code of Civil Procedure, (4) Corporations Code (including rules of the California Corporations Commissioner on corporate securities), (5) Evidence Code, (6) Insurance Code, (7) Labor Code, (8) Probate Code, (9) Uniform Commercial Code, (10) Vehicle Code.

California Corporations Code and Corporate Securities Rules; annual edition; Matthew Bender; softcover; one volume; published as part of Ballantine and Sterling.

California Corporations Code Annotated to CEB Publications; 1989; CEB; two volumes.

California Education Code Service; U.S.A. Publishing Co.; looseleaf; quarterly update; statutes and regulations pertaining to education.

Trial Attorney's Evidence Code Notebook Annotated (3d edition); 1982; CEB; looseleaf; one volume.

California Probate Code Annotated to CEB Publications; annual edition; CEB; softcover; one volume.

California Income Tax Laws; annual edition; Maxwell Macmillan; softcover; one volume; selected portions of Revenue and Taxation Code.

§7.8 STATUTES IN ELECTRONIC FORM

CD-ROM. Deering's California Codes Annotated are available in a CD-ROM format from Bancroft Whitney as part of Law Desk. West's Annotated California Codes are available in a CD-ROM format from West. (See §12.9.)

Lexis. Deering's California Codes Annotated are available on Lexis (see §12.5) in various files in the CAL library and in a combined file (CACODE) in the CAL library and the STATES library.

(1) The ALS file (Advanced Legislative Service) contains the California chapter laws from 1987 to date. The combined file (CACODE) contains chapter laws for the current year only.

(2) The CODE file contains the text of the California codified statutes, history information, and cross-references from Deering's California Codes Annotated. It does not include prefaces, outlines, annotations, tables, and non-statutory forms included in Deering's print version.

(3) The CONST file contains the text of the California Constitution, history information, and cross-references from Deering's California Codes Annotated. It does not include the annotations in Deering's print version.

(4) Statutes may also be recovered on Lexis by code section using the LEXSTAT feature.

Westlaw. West's Annotated California Codes are available on Westlaw (see §12.6) in various California libraries including annotated and unannotated versions of the codes, the California Constitution, and the California Legislative Service.

§7.9   STATUTORY INDEXES

In the annotated codes (Deering's and West), each code has its own index and the combined codes have a general index.

The general index to Deering's California Codes Annotated has a useful subject matter summary of the topics covered which lists, under each major topic, those index entries which are pertinent to the subject. For example, the general topic Consumer Protection lists twenty relevant index entries, including Bait and Switch, Lemon Law, and Pyramid Marketing Schemes as well more conventional entries such as Consumer Legal Remedies Act and Retail Installment Sales.

LARMAC Consolidated Index to the Constitution and Laws of California, published by Parker in an annual softcover edition, is a one-volume topical index to the California Constitution, codes and uncodified laws. It includes a number of particularly useful subject headings, including (1) definitions, (2) popular titles of acts, (3) uniform acts by name, and (4) counties, cities and special districts by name.

§7.10   CODE NUMBERING

While each California code may be divided into divisions, parts, chapters and articles, the basic unit of statutory law is the section (§). Statutes are generally referred to by code name and section number. The term "statute" is used fluidly, sometimes to refer to a single section of a code, sometimes to a chapter or part. An example is the marketable record title statute, consisting of Civil Code §880.020 et seq. At times, especially where an area of law is revised or a uniform act is adopted, the Legislature gives a consecutive group of statutes a general name. Some examples are:

(1)   The Trust Law (Probate Code §15000 et seq.)
(2)   The Enforcement of Judgments Law (Code of Civil Procedure §680.010 et seq.)
(3)   The Revised Limited Partnership Act (Corporations Code §15611 et seq.)

The names of the codes and the numbers of statutes are official. With some exceptions, the section headings are unofficial, that is, written by the publisher. They are not part of the law.

Statutes may be subdivided - commonly (a), (b), (c) - less commonly (1), (2), (3). Subdivisions are expressed in parentheses, since many older statutes use a combination of numbers and letters for the section number. Thus, §403(a) and §403a are different statutes. Some illustrative section numbers are: 163, 337a, 502.7,

428.10, 710.060. The more recent practice is to use decimal numbers.

§7.11   PRIOR LAW AND FORMER SECTION

In the best of all possible worlds, the Legislature would use a single statutory section number only once, and retire numbers that are removed from use. Unfortunately, section numbers are sometimes reused and statutes are sometimes moved from one location to another, and the numbers are changed. Occasionally, through oversight, there are two different statutes with the same number at the same time. When this happens, the Legislature usually renumbers one of them in the next legislative session. Thus, (1) a citation may be to an earlier statute of the same number (not necessarily the same subject matter), and (2) a citation may be to a section which has been relocated (and possibly changed along the way).

Example: C.C.P. 437 was enacted in 1872, amended four times in later years, and repealed in 1971. In 1982, the Legislature enacted a new C.C.P. 437 on a slightly different topic.

The annotated codes include notes indicating the following:

(1)   Prior law: The predecessor provision to the one appearing in the current code.
(2)   Former section: The disposition of a statute that, at a prior time, used the same section number as the material in the present code.

The age of a citation may help sort out these difficulties. If §100 in the current code was enacted in 1975, an earlier case which cites §100 must refer to an earlier statute with the same number.

Example: A 1968 case cites California Health & Safety Code §11680. A statute in the current code uses that number, but was enacted in 1982. The former section note under current §11680 indicates that the statute cited in 1968 is similar to present Health & Safety Code §11500. In the current code, the prior law note under §11500 indicates that present §11500 is based on former §11680. The amendment notes will reveal how the present statute differs from its predecessor.

For a statutory citation that can't be found in the current code, check the beginning or end of chapters or divisions of the present code for a table showing the disposition of former sections.

§7.12   EFFECTIVE DATE OF CALIFORNIA LEGISLATION

General Rule. Statutes enacted in one calendar year, generally become effective on January 1st of the following year, provided that 90 days have elapsed since the end of the legislative session. (This partly explains why the Legislature scrambles to conclude its business by the end of September; the Legislature generally reconvenes in December.)

Accelerated Effective Date. A statute may take effect on the date it is filed with the Secretary of State, if it is an urgency measure (the Legislature states that passage is urgent), a statute calling an election, a statute levying a tax, or a statute making an appropriation for current expenses. Income tax measures often apply to taxable years beginning on or after January 1st of the year of enactment.

Delayed Operative Date. A statute, though in effect, may, by its own terms or by a later enacted statute, delay the operation of its provisions until a stated contingency or specified time. Thus, for example, a statute enacted in one year may not become operative until July 1st of the following year, or may become operative only if Congress acts in a specified way. Often the operative date of a comprehensive act (like reenactment of the Probate Code) is delayed to give practitioners time to become familiar with the new law.

Resolutions. Joint and concurrent resolutions take effect on the date they are filed with the Secretary of State.

Initiatives, Referenda, and Constitutional Amendments. These take effect on the day after the election at which they are passed by the voters, unless the measure provides otherwise.

§7.13   POPULAR NAME TABLES

Popular name tables identify statutes (and well known cases) by popular name or statutory short title.   They are arranged alphabetically by name and generally provide session law and code section citations for federal and state statutes.

In USCS, the popular name table (Table of Acts by Popular Name) is in one of the hardcover tables volumes.   It is supplemented by a pocket part and by periodic softcover pamphlets called Cumulative Later Case and Statutory Service.

In USCA, the popular name table (Popular Name Table of Acts of Congress) is in the last volume of the multivolume softcover general index.   It is supplemented by a softcover pamphlet containing an Alphabetical Table of Names and a Public Law Classification Table.

In Deering's California Codes Annotated, the popular name table is at the beginning of the general index.   In West's California Codes, the table is at the end of the general index. In both sets, many popular names are included in the general index.

Shepard's popular name table is Shepard's Acts and Cases by Popular Name - Federal and State; 2 volumes; 1986; softcover supplement.

§7.14   TIPS FOR FINDING STATUTES

(1) If the citation is known, use the name or number of the code, the outline, and the section number to find the statute in USCS or USCA (for federal statutes) and Deering's or West (for California statutes).

(2) If the popular name of the statute is known, use the popular name table in USCS, USCA or Shepard's (for federal statutes) or the index of Deering's, West, or LARMAC under the popular name (for California statutes).

(3) If the specific title or code can be identified by the topic of the statute, look for key words in the index to that specific title or code. If the specific title or code cannot be identified, use the general index.

(4) If the statute is recent, check the advance legislative service that accompanies the annotated code. Check carefully, because advance pamphlets may not be cumulative.

(5) Generally, use an annotated code. Always check the pocket part for amendments and repeals after the date of publication of the bound volume. If one publisher is unhelpful, switch to the competition.

(6) Use a CD-ROM product or an online service to word search the statutes.

§7.15   NUMBERING OF PROPOSITIONS

Generally, California propositions are numbered and local propositions are lettered. At one time, state, propositions were numbered beginning with one at each election. To avoid confusion, the system was changed in 1982. Propositions are now numbered sequentially for twenty years. The current numbering period ends in 2002.

Proposition 13 refers to the property tax limitation of 1978, Cal. Const., Art XIII A.

§7.16   UNIFORM LAWS

To encourage uniformity in the statutory law of the states, the National Conference of Commissioners on Uniform State Laws has adopted many uniform and model acts and recommended that they be enacted by the states. The most successful recommendation is the Uniform Commercial Code, portions of which have been enacted in all states.

Uniform acts and codes adopted by the commissioners are published in Uniform Laws Annotated (Master edition) (ULA); West; approximately 28 hardcover volumes (green) numbered 1 to 15 with some A and B volumes; annual pocket parts and softcover pamphlet supplements; periodic replacement volumes. The set is also available online from Westlaw (ULA database).

For each act, the volume includes (1) a detailed outline, (2) introductory notes, (3) the text of the act and official comments, (4) a table of jurisdictions adopting the act, (5) notes of decisions, (6) library references, and (7) notation of action in the adopting jurisdictions (telling how the version adopted in each state varies from the official text of the uniform act).

The set is accompanied by an annual softcover pamphlet called Directory of Uniform Acts and Codes. It includes (1) an alphabetical list of acts showing their location in the set, (2) an alphabetical list of states, listing acts adopted in each state, and (3) a topical index with cross-references to the various acts. Two additional pamphlets include (1) Model Sentencing and Correction Act, and (2) Uniform Rules of Criminal Procedure and related ABA Standards for Criminal Justice.

Uniform Acts also appear in the annual Martindale Hubbell Law Digest (see §9.13). A record of the uniform acts adopted by each state is included in the Am.Jur. Deskbook and the Legal Researcher's Desk Reference (see §9.14).

Citation: Publication / name of uniform act / section
         U.L.A. (Master ed); Uniform Reciprocal Enforcement
         of Support Act, §1.

§7.17   UNIFORM ACTS ADOPTED IN CALIFORNIA

California has enacted the following uniform acts:

(1) Act on blood Tests to Determine Paternity (Evidence Code 890 et seq.) [Family Code 7550 et seq. after 1/1/94]

(2) Act to Secure Attendance of Witnesses From Without a State in Criminal Proceedings (Penal Code 1334 et seq.)

(3) Aircraft Financial Responsibility Act (Public Utilities Code 24330 et seq.)

(4) Anatomical Gift Act (Health and Safety Code 7150 et seq.)

(5) Child Custody Jurisdiction Act (Civil Code 5150 et seq.) [Family Code 3400 et seq. after 1/1/94]

(6) Civil Liability for Support Act (Civil Code 241 et seq.)

(7) Commercial Code (Uniform Commercial Code 1 et seq.)

(8) Common Trust Fund Act (Financial Code 1564)

(9) Controlled Substances Act (Health and Safety Code 11000 et seq.)

(10) Criminal Extradition Act (Penal Code 1547 et seq.)

(11) Criminal Statistics Act (Penal Code 13010 et seq.)

(12) Determination of Death Act (Health and Safety Code 7180.)

(13) Division of Income for Tax Purposes Act (Revenue and Taxation Code 25120 et seq.)

(14) Divorce Recognition Act (Civil Code 5000 et seq.) [Family Code 2090 et seq. after 1/1/94]

(15) Durable Power of Attorney Act (Civil Code 2400 et seq.)

(16) Facsimile Signatures of Public Officials Act (Government Code 5500 et seq.)

(17) Federal Lien Registration Act (Code of Civil Procedure 2100 et seq.)

(18) Foreign Money Claims Act (Code of Civil Procedure 676 et seq.)

(19) Foreign Money-Judgments Recognition Act (Code of Civil Procedure 1713 et seq.)

(20) Fraudulent Transfer Act (Civil Code 3439 et seq.)

(21) Insurers Liquidation Act (Insurance Code 1064.1 et seq.)

(22) International Wills Act (Probate Code 6380 et seq.)

(23) Interstate Arbitration of Death Taxes Act (Revenue and Taxation Code 13820 et seq.)

(24) Interstate Compromise of Death Taxes Act (Revenue and Taxation Code 13801 et seq.)

(25) Limited Partnership Act (Corporations Code 15501 et seq.)

(26) Management of Institutional Funds Act (Probate Code 18500 et seq.)

(27) Parentage Act (Civil Code 7000 et seq.) [Family Code 7600 et seq. after 1/1/94]

(28) Partnership Act (Corporations Code 15001 et seq.)

(29) Photographic Copies of Business and Public Records as Evidence Act (Evidence Code 1550, 1551)

(30) Premarital Agreement Act (Civil Code 5300 et seq.) [Family Code 1600 et seq. after 1/1/94]

(31) Principal and Income Act (Probate Code 16300 et seq.)

(32) Reciprocal Enforcement of Support Act (Code of Civil Procedure 1650 et seq.) [Family Code 4800 et seq. after 1/1/94]

(33) Rights of Terminally Ill Act (Health and Safety Code 7185 et seq.)

(34) Simultaneous Death Act (Probate Code 220 et seq.)

(35) Single Publication Act (Civil Code 3425.1 et seq.)

(36) Statutory Form Power of Attorney Act (Civil Code 2475 et seq.)

(37) Statutory Rule Against Perpetuities (Probate Code 21200 et seq.)

(38) Supervision of Trustees for Charitable Purposes Act (Government Code 12580 et seq.)

(39) Testamentary Additions to Trusts Act (Probate Code 6300 et seq.)

(40) Trade Secrets Act (Civil Code 3426 et seq.)

(41) Transfers to Minors Act (Probate Code 3900 et seq.)

(42) Vendor and Purchaser Risk Act (Civil Code 1662)

Where the application or interpretation of a California uniform act is in issue, and California authority on point does not exist, the treatment of the uniform act by courts is other jurisdictions may be relevant and persuasive. That information is available in Uniform Laws Annotated (see §7.16).

CHAPTER 8

ADMINISTRATIVE LAW

This chapter introduces the departments and
agencies of the executive branch, regulations,
and administrative proceedings.

§8.1   In General   132
§8.2   Guides and Directories   132
§8.3   California Executive Branch   133
§8.4   Administrative Agencies   138
§8.5   Secretary of State   142
§8.6   Department of Justice   142
§8.7   Attorney General Opinions   143
§8.8   Franchise Tax Board   144
§8.9   State Board of Equalization   144
§8.10   Department of Corporations   144
§8.11   Public Utilities Commission   145
§8.12   Opinions and Services   145
§8.13   California Code of Regulations   146
§8.14   Code of Federal Regulations   148
§8.15   Finding and Updating Federal Regulations   149
§8.16   Looseleaf Services   150
§8.17   Tips for Finding Administrative Law   151

———————————

§8.1 IN GENERAL

The executive branch produces administrative law, which, broadly speaking, includes regulations, executive documents, and agency opinions, decisions, and rulings. Chronological arrangements of administrative law are often called administrative registers, while subject matter arrangements of regulations are called administrative codes.

§8.2 GUIDES AND DIRECTORIES

There following publications illustrate the many guides and directories to administrative agencies, documents, and procedures:

Paper Trails: A Guide to Public Records in California by Barbara Newcombe; 1990; Center for Investigative Reporting [(415) 543-1200]; an exceptionally useful guide to finding and understanding public records

A Public Records Primer and Investigator's Handbook by Don Ray (California edition); 1991; softcover; ENG Press [(818) 843-6397]; lists offices and sources for public records

California Journal; twelve issues a year; California Journal Press

California State Government Directory; annual; California Journal Press; looseleaf; one volume; detailed directory to state legislature, judiciary, agencies, departments, boards and commissions; quarterly updates

California Lobbyists/PACs Directory; annual; California Journal Press; one volume; individual lobbyists and their employers; registered political action committees

Roster and Government Guide; annual edition; Daily Journal Corporation; softcover; one volume; directory of California executive and legislative branches; available on disk

California Political Almanac; bi-annual edition; Daily Journal Corporation; information about legislators, lobbyists, media, executive branch, local government

Trade and Professional Associations in California: A Directory (5th edition); 1992; California Institute of Public Affairs [(916) 442-CIPA]

California Handbook: A Comprehensive Guide to Sources of Current Information and Action (6th edition); 1990; California Institute of Public Affairs

California Regulatory Law Reporter; newsletter; The Center of Public Interest Law [(619) 260-4806]

California Green Book; quarterly; Dutra Communications [(916) 447-7778]; softcover; one volume; directory of people in state and federal government, including constitutional officers, legislators, state governors, campaign consultants, and political appointees; directory of state organizations and entities, listing members and professional staff

The Lawyer's Almanac; 1990; Prentice Hall; hardcover; one volume; detailed information about state and federal government agencies and departments

National Directory of State Agencies; 1986; National Standards Association [(800) 638-8094]

§8.3   CALIFORNIA EXECUTIVE BRANCH

California's executive branch is large and complex. It encompasses hundreds of executive, administrative, and advisory agencies. Many are described in state government directories (see §8.2) and can be found in the government listings of the phone book. (An alphabetical list by key words appears in §8.4; a handful of key agencies are described in following sections.) The powers and duties of administrative agencies are set by statute or, in some cases, by the state constitution. The executive branch consists of the following:

Constitutional Officers. These officers are authorized by the California Constitution (see §7.2) and are elected by the people. Each is supported by a professional staff.

Governor
Lieutenant Governor
Treasurer
Superintendent of Public Instruction
Secretary of State
Controller
Attorney General
Insurance Commissioner

State Departments. The bulk of the executive branch consists of departments and other entities under the jurisdiction of agencies with cabinet-level directors.

(1) Business, Transportation and Housing Agency

Department of Alcoholic Beverage Control
Department of State Banking
Department of Corporations
Department of Highway Patrol
Department of Housing and Community Development
Housing Finance Agency
Department of Motor Vehicles
Department of Real Estate
Department of Savings and Loan
Office of Traffic Safety
Department of Transportation

(2) California Environmental Protection Agency

Air Resources Board
Integrated Waste Management Board
Department of Pesticide Regulation
Water Resources Control Board

(3) Health and Welfare Agency

Department of Aging
Department of Alcohol and Drug Programs
Department of Developmental Services

Emergency Medical Services Agency
Employment Development Department
Department of Health Services
Health and Welfare Data Center
Major Risk Medical Insurance Board
Department of Mental Health
Department of Rehabilitation
Department of Social Services
Department of Statewide health Planning and Development

(4)   Resources Agency

Department of Boating and Waterways
California Coastal Commission
State Coastal Conservancy
Colorado River Board of California
California Conservation Corps
Department of Conservation
Department of Fish and Game
Board of Forestry
Department of Forestry and Fire Protection
Mining and Geology Board
Department of Parks and Recreation
San Francisco Bay Conservation and Development Commission
California Tahoe Conservancy
Department of Water Resources
Wildlife Conservation Board
California Wildlife Foundation

(5)   State and Consumer Services Agency

Building Standards Commission
Department of Consumer Affairs
Department of Fair Employment and Housing
State Fire Marshall
Franchise Tax Board
Department of General Services
California Museum of Science and Industry
State Personnel Board
Public Employees Retirement System
State Teachers Retirement System
Department of Veterans Affairs

(6)   Trade and Commerce Agency

        California Office of Tourism
        California Film Commission
        World Trade Commission

(7)   Youth and Adult Correctional Agency

        Department of Corrections
        Board of Prison Terms
        Youth Authority
        Youthful Offender Parole Board

    Special Offices. A number of special offices exist, some of which report directly to constitutional officers.

        Department of Finance
        Office of Administrative Law
        Office of California-Mexican Affairs
        Governor's Office of Community Relations
        Office of Criminal Justice Planning
        Department of Economic Opportunity
        Office of Emergency Services
        Office of International Affairs
        Department of Personnel Administration
        Office of Planning and Research

    Boards, Commissions, and Bureaus. A number of additional entities exist in the executive branch. Many are independent or quasi-independent, either elected or appointed.

        Board of Accountancy
        Commission on Aging
        Agricultural Labor Relations Board
        Alcoholic Beverage Control Appeals Board
        State Athletic Commission
        Arts Council
        Bureau of Automotive Repair
        Board of Behavioral Science Examiners
        California State University
        Board of Chiropractic Examiners
        Community Colleges
        Contractors State License Board

State Board of Control
Board of Dental Examiners
Developmental Disabilities Council
State Board of Education
Energy Commission
Board of Equalization
California Exposition and State Fair Board
Fair Employment and Housing Commission
Fair Political Practices Commission
Fish and Game Commission
Department of Food and Agriculture
Horse Racing Board
Department of Industrial Relations
Industrial Welfare Commission
State Library
Lottery Commission
California Maritime Academy
Medical Assistance Commission
Medical Board of California
Military Department
Native American Heritage Commission
Board of Optometry
Osteopathic Medical Board of California
Board of Pharmacy
Postsecondary Education Commission
Prison Industry Authority
State Public Defender
Public Employment Relations Board
Public Utilities Commission
Reclamation Board
Board of Registered Nursing
Seismic Safety Commission
Commission on State Government Organization and Economy
State Lands Commission
Commission on the Status of Women
Student Aid Commission
Commission on Teacher Credentialing
Transportation Commission
Unemployment Insurance Appeals Board
University of California
Water Commission
Workers' Compensation Appeals Board

§8.4   ADMINISTRATIVE AGENCIES

The following selective list of California administrative agencies is arranged alphabetically by key word:

Accountancy, Board of
Acupuncture Examining Committee
Administrative Hearings, Office of
Administrative Law, Office of
Aging, Department of
Agricultural Labor Relations Board
Air Resources Board
Alcohol and Drug Programs, Department of
Alcoholic Beverages Control Appeals Board
Alcoholic Beverage Control, Department of
Alternate Energy Source Financing Authority
Apprenticeship Standards, Division of
Architect, Office of the State
Architectural Examiners, Board of
Arts Council, California
Athletic Commission
Auctioneer Commission
Automotive Repair, Bureau of
Banking, State Department of
Barber Examiners, Board of
Behavioral Science Examiners, Board of
Boating and Waterways, Department of
Building Standards Commission
Business, Transportation and Housing Agency
CAL-OSHA Appeals Board
CAL-OSHA Division of Occupational Safety and Health
CAL-OSHA Standards Board
Cemetery Board
Chiropractic Examiners, Board of
Coastal Commission, California
Coastal Conservancy, State
Collection and Investigative Services, Bureau of
Colorado River Board
Commerce, Department of
Community Colleges, California
Conservation, Department of
Consumer Affairs, Department of

Contractors' State License Board
Controller's Office, State
Corporations, Department of
Corrections, Board of
Corrections, Department of
Cosmetology, Board of
Dental Examiners, Board of
Developmental Services, Department of
Economic Development, Commission for
Economic Opportunity, Office of
Education, Department of
Engineers, Board of Registration for Professional
Educational Facilities Financing Authority, California
Electronic and Appliance Repair, Bureau of
Emergency Medical Services Authority
Emergency Services, Office of
Employment Development, Department of
Energy Resources Conservation and Development Commission
Environmental Affairs Agency
Exposition and State Fair, California
Fair Employment and Housing Commission
Fair Employment and Housing, Department of
Fair Political Practices Commission
Finance, Department of
Fire Marshal, Office of the State
Fish and Game Commission
Fish and Game, Department of
Food and Agriculture, Department of
Forestry, Board of
Forestry and Fire Protection, Department of
Franchise Tax Board
Funeral Directors and Embalmers, Board of
General Services, Department of
Geologists and Geophysicists, Board of Registration for
Governor's Office
Guide Dogs for the Blind, State Board of
Health and Welfare Agency
Health Facilities Financing Authority, California
Health Planning and Development, Office of Statewide
Health Professions, Division of Allied
Health Services, Department of
Hearing Aid Dispensers Examining Committee
Highway Patrol, Department of California

Home Furnishing and Thermal Insulation, Bureau of
Horse Racing Board, California
Housing and Community Development, Department of
Housing Bond Credit Committee
Housing Finance Agency, California
Industrial Accidents, Division of
Industrial Development financing Advisory Agency, California
Industrial Relations, Department of
Industrial Welfare Commission
Insurance, Department of
Justice Department (Attorney General)
Labor Standards Enforcement, Division of
Labor Statistics and Research, Division of
Lands Commission, State
Landscape Architects, Board of
Law Revision Commission
Library, California State
Lieutenant Governor, Office of
Local Agency Security, Administration of
Local Assistance, Office of
Maritime Academy, California
Medical Assistance Commission, California
Medical Quality Assurance, Board of
Mental Health, Department of
Mining and Geology Board, State
Motor Vehicles, Department of
Museum of Science and Industry
Narcotic Addict Evaluation Authority
Nursing Home Administrators, Board of Examiners of
Opticians, Registered Dispensing
Optometry, State Board of
Osteopathic Examiners, Board of
Parks and Recreation, Department of
Peace Officer Standards and Training
Personnel Administration, Department of
Personnel Board, State
Personnel Services, Bureau of
Pharmacy Board, California State
Physical Therapy Examining Committee
Physician's Assistant Examining Committee
Pilot Commissioners, Board of
Planning and Research, Office of
Podiatric Medicine, Board of

Pollution Control Financing Agency, California
Polygraph Examiners, Board of
Prison Terms, Board of
Procurement, Office of
Psychology, Board of
Public Defender, State
Public Employees Retirement System
Public Employment Relations Board
Public Utilities Commission
Real Estate and Design Services, Office of
Real Estate, Department of
Reclamation Board
Registered Nursing, Board of
Rehabilitation, Department of
Resources Agency
Respiratory Care Examining Committee
San Francisco Bay Conservation and Development Commission
Santa Monica Mountains Comprehensive Planning Commission
Savings and Loan, Department of
Secretary of State
Seismic Safety Commission
Shorthand Reporters, Board of Certified
Small Business Advocate
Small and Minority Business, Office of
Small Business, Office of
Social Services, Department of
Speech Pathology and Audiology Examining Committee
State Police, Office of California
Structural Pest Control Board
Student Aid Commission
Student Loan Authority
Tax Preparers Program
Teacher Credentialing, Commission on
Teachers' Retirement System, State
Transportation and Housing Agency
Transportation Commission
Transportation, Department of
Treasurer, State
Unemployment Insurance Appeals Board, California
University, Board of Trustees of the California State
Veterans Affairs, Department of
Veterinary Medicine Board
Vocational Nurse and Psychiatric Technician Examiners, Board of

Waste Management Board, California Integrated
Water Resources Control Board, State
Water Resources, Department of
Worker's Compensation Appeals Board
Youth Authority, Department of the
Youthful Offender Parole Board

§8.5   SECRETARY OF STATE

The Secretary of State has responsibility for corporate and partnership statements and documents, corporate name reservation, UCC filings, attachments, tax liens, election procedure, campaign financing, lobbyists, notaries, and many other areas. The Office of the Secretary of State has published a number of softcover pamphlets to help those dealing with the office. The Corporations Check List, for example, explains the requirements for foreign and domestic corporations, name reservation, articles of incorporation, merger, dissolution, taxes, and fees.

Corporate information filed with the Secretary of State is available on Lexis in the CAL, CORP, INCORP, STATES and COMPNY libraries ((CAINC file). Typical information includes corporate and assumed names, filing dates, names and addresses of president and resident agent. Name reservations are not available. Limited partnership information filed with the Secretary of State is available on Lexis in the CAL library (CALTP file). The CAINC and CALTP files are combined in the CASOS File.

Various California administrative forms, including forms from the Secretary of State, are available by fax from Probus Research, a San Francisco court records and retrieval firm. Fax number (415) 553-8077.

§8.6   DEPARTMENT OF JUSTICE

The Department of Justice operates under the direction of the Attorney General, the state's chief lawyer and chief law enforcement officer. The department represents the state in civil and criminal appeals, and counsels state officials, commissions, and boards. The department also supervises charitable and non-profit entities and trusts, supports consumer protection programs, and provides state-wide support for law enforcement.

§8.7   ATTORNEY GENERAL OPINIONS

The Attorney General of California is authorized to issue legal opinions in response to questions by state and local agencies. Some recent examples: (1) May schools use metal detectors to deter possession of weapons? (2) May a city ban RV parking on private property? (3) May a homeowners association have an adults only swimming pool? Each opinion is given an identifying number, although the numbering system has changed over the years. Current numbering identifies the year and month the opinion is assigned, e.g. #87-106 refers to the 6th opinion assigned in January of 1987. Because opinions are not necessarily published in order assigned, they are cited by volume and page number: 73 Ops. Cal. Atty Gen. 153. Opinions are available in the following sources:

(1)   <u>Print</u>. Opinions of the Attorney General of California; 1961; Matthew Bender; hardcover (buff); 73 volumes through 1990; additional volume annually, monthly advance sheets. Each volume includes (1) the text of opinions, (2) an index, (3) table of opinions cited, and (4) table of statutes cited. Two companion volumes are (1) 30 year cumulative index and tables: 1943-72, and (2) 10 year cumulative index and tables: 1973-1982.

(2)   <u>Microfilm</u>. Oceana Publications; Microfiche - William S. Hein & Co.

(3)   <u>Lexis</u>. Opinions from 1977 to date are available in the CAL library (AG and AGCASE files) and the STATES library (various files).

(4)   <u>Summaries</u>. The Sacramento Digest (a feature of newspapers published by the Daily Journal) summarizes attorney

general opinions in a monthly report. The advance sheet to West's California Reporter summarizes attorney general opinions weekly.

§8.8   FRANCHISE TAX BOARD

The California Franchise Tax Board (FTB) administers the personal income tax and bank and corporate taxes as well as several other tax programs. Rulings of the Franchise Tax Board from 1958 to date with respect to the administration of the corporate franchise tax, the corporate income tax and the personal income tax are available on Lexis in the CAL library (CALFTB, CALTAX, CASES, AGCASE files) and in the STATES, STTAX, and FEDTAX libraries (various files).

§8.9   STATE BOARD OF EQUALIZATION

The California State Board of Equalization hears appeals from taxpayer audits and appeals from Franchise Tax Board decisions involving personal income tax and bank and corporate taxes. It also administers property tax, sales and use taxes, and various business taxes. Decisions, orders, and opinions of the Board of Equalization from 1930 to date are available on Lexis in the CAL library (CALSBE CALTAX, CASES, AGCASE files) and in the STATES, STTAX, and FEDTAX libraries (various files). Sales and use tax information is available in the CAL library (CASALE file).

§8.10   DEPARTMENT OF CORPORATIONS

The Department of Corporations regulates various business practices, securities, securities brokers and dealers, financial services, syndicates, and franchises, among other things. Opinions of the Department of Corporations from 1969 to date are available on Lexis is the CAL library (CALSEC, CASES and AGCASE files) and the STATES and STSEC libraries (various files). Various California administrative forms, including forms from the Department of Corporations, are available by fax from Probus Research, a San Francisco court records and retrieval firm. Fax number (415) 553-8077.

§8.11   PUBLIC UTILITIES COMMISSION

The Public Utilities Commission regulates private utilities providing telecommunications, transportation, energy and water. Decisions, rules, opinions, stipulations, and orders of the PUC from 1984 to date are available on Lexis in the CAL library (CAPUC, CASES, and AGCASE files) and the STATES and UTILTY libraries (various files).

§8.12   OPINIONS AND SERVICES

A number of publications provide access to the procedures, rules, and decisions of regulatory agencies, including the following:

California Commissioner of Corporations Official Opinions; 1969 to date; CEB; looseleaf; thirteen volumes.

California Corporate Securities Law Notebook; 1973; CEB; looseleaf; one volume; includes statutes and rules, prescribed forms, Corporations Commissioner's releases.

California Fair Political Practices Commission Notebook Service; 1975 to date; CEB; looseleaf; six volumes; includes opinions, statutes, regulations, forms, and manuals.

Fair Employment and Housing Commission Precedential Decisions; 1978 to date; CEB; looseleaf; seven volumes.

Fair Political Practices Commission's Enforcement Decisions; 1976 to date; CEB; looseleaf; three volumes.

California State Personnel Board Precedential Decisions; 1991; CEB; looseleaf.

Various California administrative forms, including forms from the Secretary of State and the Department of Corporations, are available by fax from Probus Research, a San Francisco court records and retrieval firm. Fax number (415) 553-8077.

§8.13   CALIFORNIA CODE OF REGULATIONS

The California Code of Regulations, the state counterpart to the Code of Federal Regulations (see §8.14) and the successor to the California Administrative Code, is a compilation of the regulations of state administrative agencies. Publication is supervised by the Office of Administrative Law, which enforces statutory standards for agency regulations.

The Code consists of the following titles, which are subdivided into divisions, parts, and so on. The basic unit is the section.

1 General Provisions
2 Administration
3 Food and Agriculture
4 Business Regulations
5 Education
6 Governor [no regulations]
7 Harbors and Navigation
8 Industrial Relations
9 Rehabilitative and Developmental Services
10 Investment
11 Law
12 Military and Veterans Affairs
13 Motor Vehicles
14 Natural Resources
15 Crime Prevention and Corrections
16 Professional and Vocational Regulations
17 Public Health
18 Public Revenues
19 Public Safety

20 Public Utilities and Energy
21 Public Works
22 Social Security
23 Waters
24 [reserved]
25 Housing and Community Development
26 Toxics

The California Regulatory Notice Register is a weekly publication of the Office of Administrative Law. It includes proposed regulations and final regulations filed with the Secretary of State.

The Office of Administrative Law has certified Barclays Law Publishers as the official publisher of the California Code of Regulations. The set consists of 35 looseleaf volumes (dark brown) with weekly replacement pages. The set is also available on microfiche, CD-ROM and online. The set comes with a softcover pamphlet which provides (1) a list of titles, (2) a table of contents for each title, and (3) an alphabetical list of state regulatory agencies, with addresses, phone numbers, and other information. Volume 1 contains a weekly digest of new regulations. Each title begins with a detailed outline. Titles may be purchased separately. There is a comprehensive index, updated quarterly.

The California Regulatory Law Bulletin, published by Barclays, is a weekly newsletter focusing on new and proposed regulations.

University Microfilms International (UMI) publishes an annual Comprehensive Index to the California Code of Regulations, with a periodic supplement. The index includes a subject index, the history of each code section, and tables linking the code with the California statutes.

Title 8 is available online from Fast Codes [(310) 657-4111].

Citation: title number / publication name / section
          Title 3, California Code of Regulations, §432
          3 CCR 432.

§8.14   CODE OF FEDERAL REGULATIONS

The Code of Federal Regulations (CFR) is a subject matter arrangement of federal administrative regulations. It consists of the following numbered titles:

1   General Provisions
2   [reserved]
3   The President
4   Accounts
5   Administrative Personnel
6   Economic Stabilization
7   Agriculture
8   Aliens and Nationality
9   Animals and Animal products
10   Energy
11   Federal Elections
12   Banks and Banking
13   Business Credit and Assistance
14   Aeronautics and Space
15   Commerce and Foreign Trade
16   Commercial Practices
17   Commodity and Securities Exchanges
18   Conservation of Power and Water Resources
19   Customs Duties
20   Employees' Benefits
21   Food and Drugs
22   Foreign Relations
23   Highways
24   Housing and Urban Development
25   Indians
26   Internal Revenue
27   Alcohol, Tobacco Products, and Firearms
28   Judicial Administration
29   Labor
30   Mineral Resources
31   Money and Finance: Treasury
32   National Defense
32A   National Defense, Appendix
33   Navigation and navigable Waters
34   Education
35   Panama Canal

36   Parks, Forests, and Public Property
37   Patents, Trademarks, and Copyrights
38   Pensions, Bonuses, and Veterans' Relief
39   Postal Service
40   Protection of Environment
41   Public Contracts and Property Management
42   Public Health
43   Public Lands: Interior
44   Emergency Management and Assistance
45   Public Welfare
46   Shipping
47   Telecommunication
48   [reserved]
49   Transportation
50   Wildlife and Fisheries

Regulations are divided into title, divisions and parts, which are subdivided into sections. Thus, Part 1700 may include sections 1700.1, 1700.2 etc.

CFR is published by the federal government in softcover volumes replaced each year on a rotating basis. Volumes are dated and color coded.   Two indexes are available from private publishers: (1) Code of Federal Regulations Index; hardcover; Martindale Hubbell; four volumes; (2) Index to the Code of Federal Regulations; CIS.

The Federal Register is published daily Monday through Friday. It is a chronological arrangement of federal administrative law.
Citation: Fed. Reg.

§8.15   FINDING AND UPDATING FEDERAL REGULATIONS

For each federal statute, the editorial material in the annotated codes (USCS and USCA; see §7.4) will cite pertinent regulations in the CFR (see §8.14). Notes in CFR identify the statute that authorizes the regulation and the location in the Federal Register where the regulation originally appeared.

An alphabetical list of agencies in each CFR volume tells where the agency's regulations are located in the CFR. The various indexes to the CFR provide key word access to regulations by topic.

Congress may use a statute (1) to authorize an agency to adopt regulations and (2) to limit regulations, by, e.g., specifying what the agency may consider, what it must publish, and what it may not do.

The front cover of each CFR volume lists the effective date of the revision. Subsequent changes in regulations are listed in the monthly List of CFR Sections Affected (LSA), a separate pamphlet. Changes after the effective date of the revision will be listed with a citation to the Federal Register where the change was originally published. For each month after the date of the LSA pamphlet, changes are noted in the Federal Register's Cumulative List of CFR Sections Affected. The Federal Register also has a cumulative index.

§8.16   LOOSELEAF SERVICES

A looseleaf service is published in a looseleaf format (see §2.13) and is commonly updated weekly, monthly or quarterly. Looseleaf services tend to be multivolume sets involving a highly regulated, technical subject matter (e.g., taxation) and frequently combine statutory and regulatory material (often full text) with editorial material (explanations and digests of cases and administrative rulings).

Bibliographic Guide. Legal Looseleafs in Print; Infosources Publishing [(201) 836-7072]; softcover; one volume; annual replacement volume. This index provides basis bibliographic information about legal looseleafs (title; author; publisher; number of volumes; price; frequency of publication; etc.), set forth in an alphabetical list of titles. The publication also includes (1) an index to publishers, and (2) a subject index, including geographical references. A useful companion volume is Legal Newsletters in Print (see §9.10).

Commerce Clearing House (CCH) is one of the largest publishers of looseleaf services. If has over 300 publications of one kind or another. Its concentration is in tax, employment, securities and government benefits. Volumes are generally black and called reporters (e.g., Standard Federal Tax Reporter). The numbering system is somewhat daunting for the uninitiated, but each volume includes "How to Use This Reporter." CCH generally uses whole numbers for code sections, regulations and explanations, and decimal numbers of parts of explanations and annotations.

§8.17   TIPS FOR FINDING ADMINISTRATIVE LAW

Locate material in the Code of Regulations by using the topical index or the list of agencies.

Look for citations to regulations in treatises (see §9.1) and law reviews (see §9.6) and as annotations to the relevant statutes in USCS and USCA.

Contact the relevant agency to locate specific regulations or to be added to the mailing list. If the agency has a local office, see what information is available locally. Some agencies allow visitors to use or copy material at the agency.

See if the relevant subject matter has a looseleaf service.

CHAPTER 9

COMMENTARY AND ANALYSIS

This chapter introduces the basic sources of legal commentary and analysis, including treatises, law reviews, encyclopedias, and newsletters.

§9.1	Treatises	154
§9.2	Witkin	155
§9.3	Encyclopedias	156
§9.4	Law School Texts	157
§9.5	Legal Periodicals	158
§9.6	Classification of Law Reviews	158
§9.7	Use of Law Reviews	160
§9.8	Law Reviews in California	161
§9.9	Periodical Indexes	163
§9.10	Newsletters	165
§9.11	Newsletters in California	165
§9.12	Newspapers	168
§9.13	Sources of Comparative Law	169
§9.14	Deskbooks	170

---

§9.1   TREATISES

The term "treatise" refers generally to a volume of legal commentary devoted primarily to a single topic. Treatises often begin as a single volume by one person, but may grow over the years into multivolume sets written and updated by an editorial staff. They are nearly always hardcover, may or may not be supplemented, and are frequently referred to by the last name of the original author (though current authors are sometimes also mentioned). Law school hornbooks (see §9.4) are treatises. Many of the California-specific practice works covered in chapter 10 may also be considered treatises.

Citation: Volume number / author / title / section number
1 Corbin, Contracts §100

The following works are illustrative of the standard treatises:

Anderson, Anderson on the Uniform Commercial Code
Antieau, Local Government Law
Bogert, The Law of Trusts and Trustees
Collier, Collier on Bankruptcy
Corbin, Corbin on Contracts
Couch, Couch Cyclopedia of Insurance Law
Davis, Administrative Law Treatise
Fletcher, Cyclopedia of the Law of Private Corporations
McQuillin, The Law of Municipal Corporations
Mertens, The Law of Federal Income Taxation
Moore, Moore's Federal Practice
Nimmer, Nimmer on Copyright
Powell, The Law of Real Property
Prosser, Prosser and Keeton on the Law of Torts
Scott, The Law of Trusts
Tribe, A Treatise on Constitutional Law
Wigmore, Evidence in Trials at Common Law
Williston, A Treatise on the Law of Contracts
Wright, Federal Practice and Procedure

§9.2   WITKIN

The Witkin Library, written by B.E. Witkin and published by Bancroft Whitney, consists of the following four sets of books:

(1) Summary of California Law (9th edition); 1987; Bancroft Whitney; hardcover (black); 13 volumes; annual pocket part supplement. Summary of California Law includes the following chapters:

Contracts
Agency and Employment
Workers' Compensation
Sales
Negotiable Instruments
Secured Transaction in Personal Property
Security Transactions in Real Property
Personal Property
Real Property
Torts
Constitutional Law
Taxation
Partnership
Corporations
Parent and Child
Husband and Wife
Community Property
Equity
Trusts
Wills and Probate

(2) California Procedure (3d edition); 1985; Bancroft Whitney; hardcover (black); 10 volumes; annual pocket part supplement. California Procedure includes the following chapters:

Attorneys
Courts
Jurisdiction
Actions
Pleading
Provisional Remedies

Proceedings Without Trial
Trial
Judgment
Enforcement of Judgment
Attack on Judgment in Trial Court
Extraordinary Writs
Appeal

(3)　California Evidence (3d edition); 1986; Bancroft Whitney; hardcover (black); 3 volumes; annual pocket part supplement

(4)　California Criminal Law (2d edition); 1988; Bancroft Whitney; hardcover (black); 6 volumes; annual pocket part supplement

Each of the four sets has (1) a detailed outline for each chapter, (2) a table of cases, (3) a table of statutes, rules and constitutions, (4) a parallel reference table (to earlier edition), and (5) an index. A combined index and combined tables are also available.

The Witkin library is available online from Lexis in the California library and in a CD-ROM format (called Law Desk) from Bancroft Whitney.

Works by Witkin are among the most often cited and highly regarded in California. Witkin is useful for detailed analysis, historical background, and the answers to specific substantive and procedural questions.

§9.3　　　**ENCYCLOPEDIAS**

Legal encyclopedias are multivolume, hardcover sets arranged alphabetically in chapters covering traditional legal topics. They provide a broad view of many topics, relying primarily on case law. They can be useful for a quick overview of a subject area or for comparing various approaches nationwide. Encyclopedias are kept up to day with pocket supplements and periodic replacement volumes. The two national encyclopedias are:

(1)   American Jurisprudence, 2d (Am Jur 2d); LCP (green)
(2)   Corpus Juris Secundum (CJS); West (blue)

A California encyclopedia is California Jurisprudence, Third Edition (Cal Jur 3d); 1972; Bancroft Whitney; hardcover (brown); supplemented with annual pocket supplements and periodic replacement volumes. Cal Jur 3d replaces Cal Jur 2d and includes:

(1)   Approximately 67 numbered volumes of text (some in two parts) with topical articles arranged alphabetically; each volume includes an index and a table of parallel references linking the second and third editions

(2)   A six volume general index in pamphlet binders

(3)   A five volume table of cases in a pamphlet binder

Citation Volume number / title / chapter name / section:

16A Am Jur 2d, Constitutional Law §634
16B CJS, Constitutional Law §711
13 (part 1) Cal Jur 3d, Constitutional Law §264

§9.4   LAW SCHOOL TEXTS

Traditionally, law school textbooks have been of the following types:

(1) Casebooks. A casebook is a textbook composed largely of the text of selected court opinions in a broad area of legal study, e.g., property, torts, contracts. Most casebooks also include explanatory material and discussion questions. Generally compiled by professors, casebooks serve the case method of instruction, which uses the discussion of court opinions as a vehicle for learning legal concepts. Casebooks are usually hardcover volumes, periodically revised but ordinarily without supplements. Major casebook series are published by Little Brown & Company, Foundation Press, and West.

(2) <u>Hornbooks</u>. A hornbook is a treatise (see §9.1). Based primarily on court opinions, it discusses the principles governing a broad area of legal study, e.g., property, torts, contracts. These principles are often refereed to as "black letter law." Hornbooks are generally written by professors and compliment the casebooks available in the field. As legal research tools, they can be useful in providing a conceptual framework of an area of law and in identifying key cases. Most hornbooks are hardcover (green) volumes published by West. They are commonly cited by the author's name, e.g., Prosser on Torts.

(3) <u>Outlines</u>. Law students frequently use outlines to prepare for exams. Gilbert Law Summaries, a division of Harcourt Brace, publishes outlines in approximately 35 areas of law school study, in a softcover, spiralbound format. West publishes a "nutshell" series (e.g., Estate Planning in a Nutshell) summarizing basic principles in a number of areas. Both Gilberts and Nutshells are periodically revised, but without supplements. Many bar exam review courses also produce outlines used by law students.

§9.5   LEGAL PERIODICALS

As with many concepts in the law, the notion of a legal periodical is not clearly defined. Broadly speaking, the term includes newspapers, newsletters, looseleaf services, and law reviews. Commonly, however, the term refers to law reviews. (On newspapers, see §9.12; on newsletters, see §9.10; on looseleaf services, see §8.16; on law reviews, see §9.6 et seq.)

§9.6   CLASSIFICATION OF LAW REVIEWS

Law reviews and journals (the terms have become synonymous) constitute one of the most important sources of commentary about the law. They are secondary authority, written by lawyers, judges, professors, and students. It is convenient to consider three types of reviews:

(1) <u>Academic Law Reviews</u>. Most law schools publish or aspire to publish a periodical journal or review, which is edited and published by law students. Most articles written by law professors are published in academic law reviews. Published two, four, six or eight times a year, these reviews tend to be of general interest, containing articles on many topics. Volume numbers generally reflect the academic year (fall to spring). Examples: California Law Review, Stanford Law Review.

(2) <u>Special Interest Journals</u>. Some periodicals are devoted to a single topic or area of law. They can be commercial (published by a private publisher) or academic (published by a law school). Examples: Uniform Commercial Code Law Journal; Ecology Law Review.

(3) <u>Bar Journals</u>. The journals of bar associations (see §§3.4, 3.5) and other legal groups, generally speaking, tend to be more practice oriented than academic reviews, focusing on the interests and needs of the members of the sponsoring association. Most articles written by practicing lawyers are published in bar journals. Bar journals range from high-quality scholarly works to glossy magazines (complete with restaurant reviews and advertising for expensive cars) to bar association newsletters. Bar journals tend to be published six or twelve times a year and volume numbers generally reflect the calendar year. Often, page numbers are not continuous from issue to issue within an annual volume. Examples: The California Lawyer; The Beverly Hills Bar Journal.

<u>Format</u>. Commonly, academic reviews are published throughout the year in a softcover format that uses continuous page numbering and lists the contents of each issue on the cover. Most libraries bind the issues for a single year in hardcover. If the soft covers are removed when the softcover pamphlets are bound, the tables of contents is not preserved. A cumulative index is frequently included in the final issue of the year.

<u>Citation</u>. Law reviews are cited by volume (the issues for a single year), name of review, and beginning page number of the relevant article. If page numbering is not continuous from issue to issue, the citation should include the month or number of the issue as well. The name of the author (but not student authors) and the title of the article are also usually given.

Example: Hanft, Legal Research; Daydream or Nightmare?, 100 Harv. L. Rev. 732.

§9.7   USE OF LAW REVIEWS

Law review pieces fit these common categories:

(1)   _Article_: A featured article, generally written by a professor, judge, or lawyer.

(2)   _Student Note or Comment_: A relatively short topical article written by a law student.

(3)   _Case Note or Comment_: A short article, generally student written, focusing on a recent case.

(4)   _Legislative Survey_: A synopsis of recent legislative changes.

(5)   _Symposium_: A series of articles published together and related to the same general topic; often the text of papers presented at a conference.

(6)   _Book Review_: A review of a recent publication.

Law review articles can be broad or narrow in scope, objective or persuasive in tone, analytical or practical in focus. As a research tool, a good article on point can be invaluable. It will review the legal sources available on the topic and provide relevant references to both primary and secondary authority. If easy to read and comprehend, so much the better. Some tips:

(1)   Often the most valuable material in an article has been relegated to the footnotes. They should not be overlooked.

(2)   Because of the shorter lead time for periodicals than for books, law review articles often have more current information or are devoted to "cutting edge" topics. Tips about coping with recent legislation, for example,

will probably be found first in law reviews, looseleafs, or newsletters.

(3) Law reviews are not supplemented, and become immediately dated. In addition, articles typically review and cite the existing legal literature. Thus, the best research strategy is often to find the most recent treatment of a topic and work backward.

(4) Selected law reviews can be Shepardized in Shepard's Law Review Citations; 1986; two volumes; with hardcover supplement.

§9.8   LAW REVIEWS IN CALIFORNIA

Over sixty law reviews are published in California. An alphabetical list is included as an appendix to California Government Publications and Legal Resources. Law reviews in California include the following (with initial year of publication):

American Journal of Comparative Law (Berkeley)
Asian Law Journal (Berkeley) (1993)
Asian-American and Pacific Islands Law Journal (UCLA) (1993)
Berkeley Women's Law Journal
Beverly Hills Bar Journal (1967)
Black Law Journal (UCLA) (now National Black Law Journal)
California Law Review (Berkeley) (1912)
California Lawyer (formerly California State Bar Journal) (1926)
California Western International Law Journal
California Western Law Review (1965)
Chicano Law Review (UCLA)
COMM/ENT (Hastings; Communications and Entertainment)
Comparative Labor Law (UCLA)
Criminal Justice Journal (Western State University)
Ecology Law Quarterly (Berkeley) (1971)
Federal Communications Law Journal (UCLA)
Glendale Law Review (1976)
Golden Gate University Law Review (1971)
Hastings Constitutional Law Quarterly (1974)

Hastings International and Comparative Law Review
Hastings Law Journal (1949)
High Technology Law Journal (Berkeley)
Industrial Relations Law Journal (Berkeley) (1976)
International Tax and Business Lawyer (Berkeley)
Journal of Comparative Legal Issues (University of San Diego)
Journal of Juvenile Law (University of LaVerne)
Journal of Law and Environment (University of Southern California)
La Raza Law Journal (Berkeley)
Los Angeles Lawyer (formerly Los Angeles Bar Journal) (1925)
Lincoln Law Review (1965)
Loyola of Los Angeles International and Comparative Law Journal
Loyola of Los Angeles Law Review (1968)
National Black Law Journal (UCLA) (formerly Black Law Journal)
Pacific Law Journal (1970)
Pepperdine Law Review (1973)
San Diego Law Review (1964)
San Fernando Valley Law Review (1977)
Santa Clara Computer and High Technology Law Journal
Santa Clara Law Review (1961)
Southern California Interdisciplinary Law Journal
Southern California Law Review (1927)
Southwestern University Law Review (1971)
Stanford Environmental Law Journal
Stanford Journal of International Law
Stanford Law Review (1948)
Transnational Lawyer (University of the Pacific)
U.C. Davis Law Review (1969)
U.C.L.A. Journal of Environmental Law and Policy (1980)
U.C.L.A. Law Review (1953)
U.C.L.A. Pacific Basin Law Journal
University of San Francisco Law Review (1966)
University of San Francisco Maritime Law Journal
University of West Los Angeles Law Review (1969)
Western Legal History (9th Judicial Circuit Historical Society)
Western State University Law Review (1972)
Whittier Law Review (1978)

Many law reviews are available on microfiche or microform. Two of the largest distributors are University Microfilms International (UMI) and Fred B. Rothman & Co. Rothman also stocks back issues in print format of over 200 legal periodicals. (For law reviews available online from Lexis and Westlaw, see §§12.5, 12.6.)

§9.9   PERIODICAL INDEXES

Individual Indexes. Often, individual law reviews are indexed annually, in an index published in the final issue for the year. On occasion, a review will provide a cumulative index. For example, in 1978, the Stanford Law Review published a cumulative index to volumes 1-30 (1948-1978).

Current Law Index. 1980 to date; Information Access Company; published monthly (softcover), cumulated quarterly (softcover), replaced each calendar year with a permanent hardcover edition (orange and black); originally one volume per year, now two volumes per year. The Current Law Index indexes hundreds of law reviews and other legal periodicals. It contains:

   (1)   A subject index (Part A).
   (2)   An author and title index (Part B).
   (3)   Table of cases, by plaintiff and defendant.
   (4)   Table of statutes (substantially treated).
   (5)   Book reviews. These are indexed under the title and author of the book reviewed and the entry includes a letter grade reflecting the reviewer's evaluation of the book.

InfoTrac and LegalTrac. 1980 to date; Information Access Company; CD-ROM databases under the collective title InfoTrac, including general interest, business and technology, and academic disciplines. The legal database, LegalTrac, indexes legal newspapers, law-related articles in the popular press, and the material in the Current Law Index.

Legal Resource Index. Available on microfilm and as a database (available on Lexis, Westlaw, Dialog and BRS); Information Access Company; content the same as LegalTrac.

Index to Legal Periodicals (ILP). 1926 to date; H.W. Wilson Company; 29 hardcover volumes (tan); published monthly (softcover), cumulated quarterly (softcover), replaced each year with a permanent hardcover edition. The early volumes each cover approximately three years. Beginning in 1979 with volume 19, each volume covers one year, from September to the following August. The index includes U.S. and foreign periodicals which regularly publish legal articles. The volumes are not cumulative. Each volume contains the following:

(1) An alphabetical list of the periodicals indexed and an alphabetical list of their abbreviations.

(2) A list of subject headings.

(3) A subject and author index. Student authors are omitted. Articles, case notes, legislative notes, biographies and bibliographies are subject to length restrictions (short ones are omitted).

(4) A table of cases, by plaintiff and defendant.

(5) A table of statutes, alphabetical by jurisdiction.

(6) An index of book reviews, by title and author of the book.

Index to Periodical Articles Related to Law. Compiled by Mersky and Jacobstein; 1958 to date; Glanville Publishers; cumulated in four hardcover volumes (black) covering 1958-1988. This publication is a selective index to law-related articles in publications not covered in the Index to Legal Periodicals, the Current Law Index or the Index to Foreign legal Periodicals. Volumes 1 and 2 contain a subject index and a list of subject headings. Volumes 3 and 4 contain an author index, a list of periodicals, and an appendix listing other indexes covering articles related to law.

Law Review Access. Weekly; Law Review Access (University of Connecticut Law Library); loose pages with copies of the tables of contents of law reviews received by the University of Connecticut Law Library; for a fee, a copy of any article cited in the Law Review Access, Current Law Index, Legal Resource Index, or Index to Legal Periodicals may be ordered.

Shepard's Law Review Citations. 1957 to date; shows where selected law reviews have been cited in later authorities.

§9.10   NEWSLETTERS

Newsletters are published by private publishers and by many special interest bar association committees and sections. They generally include lead articles, summaries of recent cases and legislation, practical advice, and notices. They are generally more timely than books and law reviews and can be especially useful for recent developments and practice pointers.

Legal Newsletters in Print: Infosources Publishing [(201) 836-7072]; softcover; one volume; annual replacement volume. This index provides basis bibliographic information about legal newsletters (title; author; publisher; date; frequency of publication; format), in an alphabetical list of titles. The publication also includes (1) an index to publishers, (2) a subject index, including geographical references, and (3) a list of subject headings. A useful companion volume is Legal Looseleafs in Print (see §8.16).

§9.11   NEWSLETTERS IN CALIFORNIA

Newsletters of note in California include the following:

California State Bar Section	Newsletter
Antitrust & Trade Regulation	Competition
Business Law	Business Law News
Criminal Law	Criminal Law News
Estate Planning, Trust and Probate	Estate Planning, Trust and Probate News
Family Law	Family Law News
General Practice	The General Practitioner
Intellectual Property	New Matter
International Law	International Practitioner
Labor & Employment Law	California Labor & Employment Law Quarterly
Law Practice Management	The Bottom Line
Legal Services	Legal Services Section News
Litigation	California Litigation

Public Law	Public Law News
Real Property Law	California Real Property Journal
Taxation	California Tax Lawyer
Workers' Compensation	Workers' Compensation Quarterly

Bancroft Whitney

(1) Alternative Dispute Resolution Newsalert (California Edition); six issues a year

(2) Gilfix California Elder Law Newsalert; six issues a year

(3) Miller and Starr California Real Estate Newsalert; six issues a year

CEB

(1) California Business Law Reporter; eight issues a year

(2) California Business Law Practitioner; four issues a year

(3) Civil Litigation Reporter; eight issues a year

(4) Estate Planning and California Probate Reporter; six issues a year

(5) Land Use Forum; four issues a year

(6) Real Property Law Reporter; eight issues a year

Matthew Bender

(1) California Criminal Defense Practice Reporter; twelve issues a year

(2) California Employment Law Reporter; twelve issues a year

(3) California Family Law Monthly; twelve issues a year

(4) California Real Estate Reporter; twelve issues a year

Shepard's

(1) California Construction Law Reporter; twelve issues a year

(2) California Environmental Law and Regulation Reporter; twelve issues a year

(3) California Insurance Law and Regulation Reporter; twelve issues a year

(4) California Land Use Law and Policy Reporter; twelve issues a year

(5) California Tort Reporter; ten issues a year

(6) California Water Law and Policy Reporter; twelve issues a year

Law Firms

(1) Environmental Law Update; Orrick, Harrington & Sutcliffe
(2) Legal Update on California Insurance Law Issues; Hancock, Rothert & Bunshoft
(3) Insurance Case Commentary; Lewis, D'Amato, Brisbois & Bisgaard
(4) State and Local Tax Insights; Morrison & Foerster
(5) Employee Benefits Update; Brobeck, Phleger & Harrison
(6) Labor & Employment Update; Brobeck, Phleger & Harrison
(7) Employee Benefits and Executive Compensation; Morrison & Foerster

Other Publishers

(1) Barclays Labor Law Bulletin (California Edition); twelve issues a year
(2) Barclays Business Law Bulletin (California Edition); twelve issues a year
(3) BNA California Employee Relations Report; 25 issues a year
(4) BNA California Safety and Health Report; 25 issues a year
(5) California Civil Law Reporter (Law Alert); La Jolla Legal Publications [(800) 498-3991]; 26 issues a year
(6) California Criminal Law Reporter; La Jolla Legal Publications; 26 issues a year
(7) California Environmental Insider; California Environmental Publications [(415) 456-4811; 26 issues a year
(8) California Family Law Report (12 issues a year) and California Family Law First Alert (48 issues a year); California Family Law Report, Inc.
(9) California Regulatory Law Reporter; Center for Public Interest Law
(10) CTLA (California Trial Lawyers Association) Forum
(11) Ninth Circuit Criminal Law Reporter
(12) California Labor and Employment Alert for All California Employers; Castle Publications [(818) 708-3208]

§9.12   NEWSPAPERS

There are over a dozen major legal newspapers in California. They are listed in CEB, Probate Workflow Manual. Generally, they provide the following:

(1)   News of interest to the legal community
(2)   Local bar association news
(3)   Court calendars (state and federal courts)
(4)   Calendar of coming events, including MCLE programs
(5)   Display and classified advertising
(6)   Legal notices - e.g., fictitious business name
(7)   Synopsis of recent state and federal cases

The most widely used include the following:

Daily Journal. Three editions (The Los Angeles Daily Journal, the San Francisco Banner Daily Journal, and The Daily Recorder [Sacramento]), with the following features:

(1)   Issues Monday through Friday
(2)   Sacramento Digest - a weekly supplement including (1) a digest of bills (prepared by Legitech), (2) a summary of legislative action, (3) a summary of recent regulatory changes (prepared by Barclays), (4) a calendar of administrative and legislative meetings, (5) notice of recent reports and publications, and (6) guest columns.
(3)   Daily Appellate Report - the text of recent cases.
(4)   Daily Journal Report - a monthly supplement including (1) full length articles on various topics, and (2) abstracts of law review articles of general interest.

Recorder. San Francisco edition with the following features:

(1)   Issues Monday through Friday
(2)   California Daily Opinion Service - the text of recent cases.
(3)   The Recorder is available online in full text on Lexis: Nexis library, REDRDR file; LGLNEW library, REDRDR file.

<u>National Law Journal</u>. A national, weekly legal newspaper, published by the New York Law Publishing Company; includes news, features, advertising, a brief digest of selected recent decisions (state and federal), and a topical list of recent books and law review articles of interest; available online from Lexis and Westlaw.

§9.13 SOURCES OF COMPARATIVE LAW

For answers to questions about the law in other jurisdictions, for example, the drinking age in Montana or a summary of Japanese copyright law, the following are available:

(1) Martindale Hubbell Law Digest, published annually in three hardcover volumes, two for the United States and one for foreign countries. The set includes a summary of law in various areas for each jurisdiction and selected international conventions. It also indicates which states have adopted uniform and model acts and includes the text of those acts. (On uniform laws, see §7.16.)

(2) Subject Compilation of State Laws: An Annotated Bibliography; volume 1 (1960-1979); volume 2 (1979-1983); volume 3 (1983-1985); volume 4 (1985-1988); annotated guide to published topical sources, arranged alphabetically by subject matter; author and publisher index.

(3) National Survey of State Laws; 1992; Gale.

(4) The Lawyer's Almanac, Shepard's Lawyer's Reference Manual, and other deskbooks (see §9.14).

A number of specialized comparative guides are also published, for example, Punitive Damages, A State-by-State Guide to Law and Practice: West; available in print and on Westlaw (PUNITIVE).

§9.14   DESKBOOKS

A deskbook is typically a one or two volume general legal reference. The following are illustrative:

American Jurisprudence Deskbook; LCP; one volume; detailed information about federal and state government; statistical and geographical information; research and practice aids; historical documents.

Law and Legal Information Directory (8th edition); 1992; Gale Research Inc.; hardcover; two volumes. This publication provides national information about legal organizations and topics, including:

(1) Federal and state courts
(2) Law schools, continuing legal education, bar associations and bar exams
(3) Federal regulatory agencies, listed by name, acronym and key word
(4) Special libraries, research centers, and publishers
(5) Legal periodicals (including a key word index)
(6) Referral services, legal aid offices, public defenders

The Lawyer's Almanac (10th edition); 1990; Prentice Hall hardcover; one volume; information about the legal profession, the judiciary, government departments and agencies; comparative state laws; common legal abbreviations.

Lawyer's Desk Book (9th); Prentice Hall; hardcover; one volume; detailed information about major legal topics (e.g. Corporate Formation and Operation; Personal Injury and Nofault; Real Estate Transactions); comparative state information (e.g., State Blue Sky Laws; Revocation of Wills) and financial computations (e.g., interest tables, present value, life insurance).

Lawyers Desk Reference; 1987; LCP; hardcover; two volumes; detailed information about various topics, generally tort oriented (e.g., hazardous automobile design; technical testing laboratories; safety standards and codes).

The Legal Researcher's Desk Reference; 1991; Infosources Publishing [(201) 836-7072]; one volume; softcover; detailed information about federal and state courts, agencies, and legislatures; libraries, legal publishers, legal periodicals, bar associations, and law schools.

Shepard's Lawyer's Reference Manual; a digest of state laws on approximately thirty topics; state by state information about judicial systems and government agencies and departments.

West's Legal Desk Reference; 1991; West; hardcover; one volume; dictionary, citation, bibliography, abbreviations, phone numbers and addresses.

CHAPTER 10

PRACTICE WORKS AND FORM BOOKS

This chapter identifies the major practice works and leading legal publishers in California.

§10.1	In General	174
§10.2	Bancroft Whitney	174
§10.3	CEB	175
§10.4	CEB Action Guides	176
§10.5	CEB Practice Books	177
§10.6	Matthew Bender	184
§10.7	Parker	186
§10.8	Rutter Group	188
§10.9	Other California Practice Works	189
§10.10	CLE Program Materials	192
§10.11	Self-Help Books	192

---

§10.1   IN GENERAL

Like many legal concepts, the term "practice work" is imprecise. Generally, however, the term refers to a work in which the primary focus is telling legal professionals how to do something rather than about the law. Of course, many works have jurisprudential as well as practical aspects. Frequently, practice works include sample forms. Those devoted principally to forms are called form books. Topical newsletters frequently have practice components. (On newsletters, see §9.10.)

§10.2   BANCROFT WHITNEY

Bancroft Whitney, a division of Thomson Legal Publishing, is a California-specific publisher of legal information. It is known primarily as the publisher of Witkin (see §9.2), the California Official Reports (see §5.4), and Deering's California Codes (see §7.6). Its practice works include the following:

Bancroft Whitney's California Civil Practice; 1991; pamphlet binders (black with colored highlights); separate topical modules, including Civil Procedure (five volumes), Torts (four volumes); Business (six volumes); Probate and Trusts (four volumes); other modules in process; includes forms on disk.

Miller and Starr California Real Estate (2d edition); 1989; text: nine volumes; hardcover (blue); tables and index: one volume, pamphlet binder; case digest: two volumes, pamphlet binder.

California Condominium Handbook; 1986; hardcover (brown); two volumes.

California Criminal Forms and Instructions; 1983; hardcover (green); three volumes.

California Forms, Legal and Business; 1968; hardcover (black and tan); 15 volumes.

California Personal Injury Digest; 1991; pamphlet binder (blue); two volumes.

California Trial Handbook (2d edition); 1987; hardcover (blue); one volume.

California Negotiation and Settlement Handbook; 1991; pamphlet binder (blue); one volume.

Modern California Discovery (4th edition); 1988; hardcover (blue); three volumes.

California Drunk Driving Defense; 1988; pamphlet binder (white); one volume.

California Judicial Council Forms Manual; semi-annual; softcover; one volume.

§10.3   CEB

CEB (Continuing Education of the Bar) is one of California's largest legal publishers. Its works are practice oriented and specific to California. The CEB practice library consists of the following:

(1) Action Guides. Concise procedural and transactional guides in a softcover format. The Action Guides Reference is an index to action guides in business law, criminal law, family law, real property law, estate planning and probate. (For a list of action guides, see §10.4.)

(2) Books. Hardcover, softcover, and looseleaf volumes on a wide variety of topics, generally supplemented annually. (For a list of books, see §10.5.)

(3) Computer Programs. Forms and document software; interactive video. (For forms on disk, see §12.2.)

(4) <u>Newsletters</u>. Feature articles, commentary and analysis of recent cases, new legislation, and pending litigation in selected areas; softcover format. (On newsletters, see §9.10.)

(5) <u>CLE Program Materials</u>. (See §10.10.)

(6) <u>Client Handbooks</u>. Inexpensive guides designed to be provided by lawyers to their clients. These include: (1) Americans With Disabilities Act: A Practical Guide for Employers; (2) Employment Termination Law: A Practical Guide for Employers; (3) Model Employee Handbook for the Small California Business; (4) Sexual Harassment in the Workplace: A Practical Guide for Employers

§10.4   CEB ACTION GUIDES

Approaching a Marital Dissolution
Approaching Construction Disputes
Creating Your Discovery Plan
Defending Your Client in a Misdemeanor Case (Including a DUI)
Effectively Handling Your Client Relationship
Enforcing Civil Money Judgments
Enforcing Security Interests in Personal Property
Forming and Operating S Corporations
Handling a Chapter 7 Consumer Bankruptcy
Handling a Real Estate Broker Liability Action
Handling a Real Property Foreclosure
Handling a Wrongful Termination Action
Handling Civil Appeals
Handling Civil Writs in the Courts of Appeal
Handling Claims Against Government Entities
Handling Depositions
Handling Expert Witnesses in California Courts
Handling Expert Witnesses in Federal Courts
Handling Mechanics' Liens and Related Remedies (Private Works)
Handling Public Works Remedies: Stop Notices and Payment Bonds
Handling Real Property Sales Transactions
Handling Service of Process (Serving Summons in Civil Proceedings)
Handling Subpenas
Handling Unlawful Detainers

Laying a Foundation to Introduce Evidence (Preparing and Using
    Evidence at Trial)
Making a Claim Under a Title Insurance Policy
Making a Summary Judgment Motion
Minimizing Toxics Liability When Buying Real Property and
    Businesses
Moving for Relief from an Automatic Stay in Bankruptcy
Moving to Compel Discovery and Other Discovery Motions
Obtaining Appointment of a Receiver (And Monitoring the
    Receivership)
Obtaining an Injunction
Obtaining a Writ of Attachment
Obtaining a Writ of Possession
Obtaining Discovery Initiating and Responding to Discovery
    Procedures
Obtaining Injunctions
Preparing for Trial
Removing an Action to Federal Court
Representing a Debtor in Chapter 7 Business Bankruptcy
Taking Security Interests in Personal Property
Transferring Property Without Probate
Meeting Statutory Deadlines
        Part 1 - Injury to Person and Personal Property Litigation
        Part 2 - Real Property and Land Use Litigation
        Part 3 - Contractual and Financial Injury Litigation
        Part 4 - Deadlines During and After Litigation
        Part 5 - Workers' Compensation
        Part 6 - Real Property and Commercial Transactions Deadlines
        Part 7 - Business Entities Filing Requirements and Deadlines
        Part 8 - Specialized Litigation and Transaction Deadlines
        Part 9 - Securities Transactions Deadlines
        Reference Guide to 9-Part Series

§10.5   CEB PRACTICE BOOKS

Advising California Condominium and Homeowners Associations; 1992;
hardcover; one volume; forms on disk.

Advising California Employers; 1981; hardcover; one volume.

Advising California Nonprofit Corporations; 1984; hardcover; one volume.

Advising California Partnerships (2d edition); 1988; hardcover; one volume; forms on disk.

Appeals and Writs in Criminal Cases; 1982; hardcover; one volume.

Attorney's Guide to California Construction Contracts and Disputes (2d edition); 1990; hardcover; one volume.

Attorney's Guide to California Professional Corporations (4th edition); 1987; looseleaf; one volume.

Attorney's Guide to Pension and Profit-Sharing Plans (3d edition); 1985; looseleaf; one volume.

Attorney's Guide to Trade Secrets; 1971; softcover; one volume.

Basic Personal Injury Anatomy; 1966; hardcover; one volume; not supplemented.

Business Buy-Sell Agreements; 1991; looseleaf; one volume; forms on disk.

California Administrative Hearing Practice; 1984; hardcover; one volume.

California Administrative Mandamus (2d edition); 1989; hardcover; one volume.

California Attorney's Damages Guide; 1974; softcover; one volume.

California Attorney's Fees Award Practice; 1982; hardcover; one volume.

California Automobile Insurance Law Guide; 1973; softcover; one volume.

California Breach of Contract Remedies; 1980; hardcover; one volume.

California Business Practice Forms Manual; 1992; looseleaf; two volumes; forms on disk; collects forms from other CEB business practice books.

California Civil Appellate Practice (2d edition); 1985; hardcover; one volume.

California Civil Litigation Forms Manual; 1980; looseleaf; two volumes.

California Civil Procedure Before Trial (3d edition); 1990: looseleaf; three volumes; forms on disk.

California Civil Procedure During Trial; 1982, 1984; hardcover; two volumes.

California Civil Writ Practice (2d edition); 1987; hardcover; one volume.

California Commercial Law; 1964; hardcover; two volumes.

California Condominium and Planned Development Practice; 1984; hardcover; one volume.

California Conservatorships and Guardianships; 1990; looseleaf; two volumes.

California Criminal Law Procedure and Practice; 1986; hardcover; one volume.

California Decedent Estate Practice; 1986, 1987; looseleaf; three volumes.

California Durable Power of Attorney Handbook; annual edition; softcover; one volume; forms on disk.

California Elder Law: An Advocate's Guide; 1993; looseleaf; two volumes; forms on disk.

California Eviction Defense Manual (2d edition); 1993; looseleaf; two volumes; forms on disk.

California Evidence Benchbook (2d edition); 1982; hardcover; two volumes.

California Expert Witness Guide (2d edition); 1991; looseleaf; one volume.

California Government Tort Liability Practice (3d edition); 1992; hardcover; one volume.

California Judicial Council Forms Manual: 1981; looseleaf; three volumes.

California Juvenile Court Practice; 1981; hardcover; two volumes.

California Liability Insurance Practice: Claims and Litigation; 1991; looseleaf; two volumes.

California Lis Pendens Practice; 1983; hardcover; one volume.

California Marital Termination Agreements; 1988; looseleaf; one volume; forms on disk.

California Mechanics' Liens and Other Remedies (2d edition); 1988; hardcover; one volume.

California Mortgage and Deed of Trust Practice (2d edition); 1990; hardcover; one volume.

California Personal Injury Proof; 1970; hardcover; one volume.

California Probate Workflow Manual (revised); 1989; looseleaf; two volumes.

California Real Property Financing; 1988, 1989; hardcover; two volumes.

California Real Property Practice Forms Manual; 1988; looseleaf; one volume; forms on disk; collects forms from other CEB real property practice books.

California Real Property Remedies Practice; 1982; hardcover; one volume.

California Real Property Sales Transactions; 1981; hardcover; one volume.

California Residential Landlord-Tenant Practice; 1986; hardcover; one volume.

California Search and Seizure Practice (2d edition); 1977; hardcover; one volume.

California Subdivision Map Act Practice; 1987; softcover; one volume.

California Surety and Fidelity Bond Practice; 1969; hardcover; one volume.

California Taxes (2d edition); 1988; looseleaf; two volumes.

California Title Insurance Practice; 1980; hardcover; one volume.

California Tort Damages; 1988; hardcover; one volume.

California Tort Guide (2d edition); 1979; hardcover; one volume.

California Trial Objections (2d edition); 1984; hardcover; one volume.

California Trust Administration (revised edition); 1990; looseleaf; one volume.

California Uninsured Motorist Practice; 1973; hardcover; one volume.

California Will Drafting (3d edition); 1992; looseleaf; three volumes; forms on disk.

California Workers' Compensation Practice (3d edition); 1985; hardcover; one volume.

California Workers' Damages Practice; 1985; hardcover; one volume.

California Zoning Practice; 1969; hardcover; one volume.

Civil Discovery Practice in California; 1988; hardcover; two volumes.

Civil Trials Benchbook; 1981; hardcover; one volume.

Commercial Real Property Lease Practice; 1976; hardcover; one volume; forms on disk.

Competitive Business Practices (2d edition); 1991; hardcover; one volume.

Condemnation Practice in California; 1973; hardcover; one volume.

Counseling California Corporations; 1990; hardcover; one volume.

Debt Collection Practice in California; 1987; hardcover; two volumes.

Debt Collection Tort Practice; 1971; hardcover; one volume.

Drafting Agreements for the Sale of Businesses (2d edition); 1988; hardcover; one volume; forms on disk.

Drafting California Irrevocable Living Trusts (2d edition); 1987; looseleaf; one volume.

Drafting California Revocable Living Trusts (2d edition); 1984; hardcover; one volume.

Effective Direct and Cross-Examination; 1986; hardcover; one volume.

Effective Introduction of Evidence in California; 1990; looseleaf; one volume.

Estate Planning Practice; 1987; looseleaf; two volumes.

Fee Agreement Forms Manual; 1989; looseleaf; one volume; forms on disk.

Financing California Businesses; 1976; hardcover; one volume.

Ground Lease Practice; 1971; hardcover; one volume.

Guide to California Subdivision Sales Law; 1974; softcover; one volume.

Jefferson's Synopsis of California Evidence Law; 1985; one volume.

Landslide and Subsidence Liability; 1974; softcover; one volume.

Managing an Estate Planning Practice (revised edition); 1992; looseleaf; one volume; forms on disk.

Organizing Corporations in California (2d edition); 1983; looseleaf; one volume; forms on disk.

Personal Tax Planning for Professionals and Owners of Small Businesses; 1988; hardcover; one volume.

Persuasive Opening Statements and Closing Arguments; 1988; hardcover; one volume.

Practice Under the California Family Law Act: Dissolution, Legal Separation, Nullity; annual replacement; softcover; one volume

Practicing California Judicial Arbitration; 1983; hardcover; one volume.

Proof in Competitive Business Litigation; 1993; looseleaf; one volume.

Real Property Exchanges; 1982; hardcover; one volume.

Sales and Leases in California Commercial Law Practice; 1993; looseleaf; two volumes; forms on disk.

Secured Transactions in California Commercial Law Practice; 1986; hardcover; two volumes.

Tax Aspects of California Partnerships; 1983; hardcover; one volume.

Tax Aspects of Marital Dissolutions (2d edition); 1989; CEB: softcover; one volume.

Taxation of Real Property Transfers; 1981; hardcover; one volume.

Tax Practice in California: A Guide to Federal Procedure; 1984; hardcover; one volume.

Wrongful Employment Termination Practice; 1987; hardcover; one volume.

§10.6   MATTHEW BENDER

Matthew Bender publishes many looseleaf practice works on a variety of state and federal topics. Works specifically dealing with California law are listed below. Many of them are also available on CD-ROM, in Bender's Search Master, California Library. (On CD-ROM, see §12.9.)

Ballantine and Sterling, California Corporation Laws (4th edition); 1962; looseleaf (dark blue); six volumes.

California Attorney Practice; 1986; looseleaf; three volumes.

California Civil Actions--Pleading and Practice; 1983; looseleaf (blue); five volumes.

California Closely Held Corporations: Tax Planning and Practice Guide; 1987; looseleaf; three volumes.

California Community Property with Tax Analysis; 1985; looseleaf; one volume.

California Criminal Defense Practice; 1981; looseleaf; seven volumes.

California Deposition and Discovery Practice; revised 1987; looseleaf (blue); three volumes.

California Employment Law; 1989; looseleaf (grey); four volumes.

California Employers' Guide to Employee Handbooks and Personnel Policy Manuals; 1989; one volume; looseleaf (grey); annual revisions.

California Environmental Law and Land Use Practice; 1989; looseleaf; four volumes.

California Family Law--Practice and Procedure; 1978; looseleaf (blue); seven volumes.

California Family Tax Planning (2d edition); 1966; looseleaf; two volumes.

California Forms of Pleading and Practice--Annotated; 1962; looseleaf (light blue with black); 52 volumes; supplemented five times annually; volumes numbered 1 to 14 with many A and B volumes, arranged alphabetically; general index, table of cases, table of statutes, probate and Judicial Council forms. For each topic there is a table of contents, list of definitions, general discussion of the topic, sample forms and instructions, citations to relevant statutes, decisions and rules, and points and authorities.

California Insurance Law and Practice; 1986; looseleaf (grey); four volumes.

California Intellectual Property Handbook; softcover; one volume; annual replacement volume.

California Law of Employee Injuries and Worker's Compensation; (2d edition); 1966; looseleaf; four volumes.

California Legal Forms--Transaction Guide; 1968; looseleaf (light blue with red); 28 volumes; law, procedure, and forms for basic legal and business transactions, arranged topically.

California Mechanics' Lien Law and Construction Industry Practice (5th edition); 1990; looseleaf; one volume.

California Points and Authorities; 1965; looseleaf (dark blue); 23 volumes (numbered 1 to 13 with A and B volumes), arranged alphabetically.

California Probate Practice; 1991; looseleaf (gray); four volumes; Judicial Council forms for decedents' estates in an additional volume.

California Products Liability Actions (revised edition); 1975: looseleaf; one volume.

California Public Agency Practice; 1988; looseleaf; three volumes.

California Public Sector Labor Relations; 1989; looseleaf; one volume.

California Real Estate Law and Practice; 1973; looseleaf (blue); 16 volumes.

California Taxation (2d edition); 1989; looseleaf; five volumes.

California Torts; 1985; looseleaf (blue); six volumes.

California Trial Guide; 1986; looseleaf (black); six volumes.

California Wills and Trusts Forms; looseleaf (grey); six volumes (three of text, three of forms); forms on disk.

Practice Under the California Corporate Securities Law; 1972; looseleaf; three volumes.

Workers' Compensation Law of California; softcover; annual replacement volume.

§10.7   PARKER

Parker Publications, a division of Butterworth Legal Publishers, has a number of titles related to California practice, including the following:

A Business Guide to California Small Claims Court; 1992; softcover; one volume.

California Community Property Handbook (3d edition); 1991; softcover; one volume.

California Community Property Law; 1988; looseleaf; maroon; two volumes.

California Complex Litigation Manual; 1991; looseleaf (black); one volume.

California Courtroom Evidence (3d edition); 1988; looseleaf; one volume.

California Damages: Law and Proof (4th edition); 1990; looseleaf (black); one volume.

California Insurance Disputes; 1991; looseleaf; one volume.

California Mechanics' Lien Law and Construction Industry Practice (5th edition); 1990; looseleaf (red); one volume.

California Mechanics' Lien Law Handbook (3d edition); 1992; softcover; one volume.

California Misconduct Cases (3d edition); 1991; softcover; one volume.

California Objections at Trial; 1992; softcover; one volume.

California Probate Procedure (5th edition); 1989; looseleaf (black); two volumes.

California Trial Techniques; 1991; looseleaf; one volume.

California Unemployment and Disability Compensation Programs (8th edition); 1991; parker; looseleaf; one volume.

California Unemployment Insurance Handbook; 1991; softcover; one volume.

California Uninsured Motorist Law (4th edition); 1986; looseleaf (blue); two volumes.

California White Collar Crimes; 1991; looseleaf; one volume.

California Workers' Compensation Claims and Benefits (8th edition); looseleaf; one volume.

California Workers' Compensation Law (4th edition); 1990; looseleaf (green); two volumes.

California Workers' Compensation Handbook (12th edition); 1993; softcover; one volume.

Guide to California Evidence (2d edition); 1988; looseleaf (brown); two volumes.

Labor and Employment in California; 1992; looseleaf; one volume.

§10.8   RUTTER GROUP

The Rutter Group publishes a library of looseleaf guides under the general title: California Practice Guide. Each set includes tables of cases, statues, and rules, and an index. The text is in outline form. It is usually faster to pinpoint material in the outline than to browse in the text. The library includes the following:

California Practice Guide: Alternative Dispute Resolution; 1992; looseleaf (maroon); one volume.

California Practice Guide: Bad Faith; 1986; looseleaf (brown); one volume.

California Practice Guide: Civil Appeals and Writs; 1989; looseleaf (blue); two volumes.

California Practice Guide: Civil Procedure Before Trial; 1983; looseleaf (grey); three volumes.

California Practice Guide: Civil Trials and Evidence; 1993; looseleaf (blue); three volumes.

California Practice Guide: Corporations; 1984; looseleaf (green); two volumes.

California Practice Guide: Enforcing Judgments and Debts; 1988; looseleaf (grey); two volumes.

California Practice Guide: Family Law; 1981; looseleaf (brown); three volumes.

California Practice Guide: Federal Civil Procedure Before Trial; 1989; looseleaf (orange); two volumes.

California Practice Guide: Landlord-Tenant; 1989; looseleaf (purple); two volumes.

California Practice Guide: Law Practice Management; 1992; looseleaf; one volume.

California Practice Guide: Personal Injury; 1984; looseleaf (red); two volumes.

California Practice Guide: Probate; 1986; looseleaf (dark blue); two volumes.

§10.9   OTHER CALIFORNIA PRACTICE WORKS

Association of Municipal Court Clerks

      Appeals Procedure Manual (1988)
      Civil Procedure Manual (1986)
      Civil Defaults and Default Judgments Manual
      Criminal Procedure Manual (1991)
      Small Claims Procedure Manual (1992)

CJER (see §4.17) California Judges Benchbooks

      Civil Trials; hardcover; one volume; available from CEB

      Criminal Pretrial Proceedings; 1991; softcover; one volume; available from CEB

      Criminal Trials; 1991; softcover; one volume; available from CEB

      Criminal Posttrial Proceedings; 1991; softcover; one volume; available from CEB

      Search and Seizure; 1991; softcover; one volume; available from CEB

Small Claims Court and Consumer Law; 1993 (5th edition); softcover; one volume; available from Bancroft Whitney

Felony Sentencing Handbook (1993); softcover; one volume; available from Bancroft Whitney

Shepard's

California ADR Practice Guide; 1992; one volume

California Foreclosure: Law and Practice; 1991; looseleaf; one volume

California Land Use Procedure; 1992; looseleaf; two volumes

California Construction Law Manual (4th edition); 1990; hardcover; one volume

West

California Civil Trialbook; looseleaf; one volume

California Products Liability Law and Practice; hardcover (red); one volume

California Code Forms; hardcover; 19 volumes

California Practice; hardcover (black); 18 volumes

Other Publishers

California Administrative and Antitrust Law; 1992; Butterworth Legal Publishers; looseleaf; two volumes

California Arbitration Practice Guide by Toker (2d edition); 1993; Lawpress [(800) 622-1181]

California Corporate Practice Guide (2d edition); 1985; Lawpress; looseleaf; one volume

Marsh's California Corporation Law (3d edition); 1990; Prentice Hall; looseleaf (maroon); four volumes

California Real Estate Forms and Commentaries by Cheatham and Merritt; 1984; Prentice Hall; looseleaf; one volume

Basic California Family Law Handbook by Adams and Sevitch; California Family Law Report

California Family Law Practice by Adams and Sevitch; 1991; California Family Law Report; looseleaf; two volumes; update service

California Family Law Report; monthly with weekly update called First Alert

California Hazardous Waste Management; California Environmental Publications; one volume

California State and Local Taxes; annual edition; Research Institute of America; looseleaf (maroon); three volumes

California Tax Handbook; annual edition; Maxwell Macmillan; softcover; one volume; cross-references to Prentice Hall, California State and Local Taxes

Taxing California Property (3d edition) by Ehrman and Flavin; 1989; Clark Boardman Callaghan; looseleaf (green); two volumes

Guidebook to California taxes; annual edition; CCH; softcover; one volume; also available on disk

California Tax Guide; CCH; looseleaf; monthly update

California Medi-Cal Guide; CCH; looseleaf; monthly update

Handbook of California Remedies by Simmons; 1993; Little Brown; hardcover; one volume

Caskey's Benchguide to California Search and Seizure Cases; [(800) 479-6062]

§10.10   CLE PROGRAM MATERIALS

Providers of Continuing Legal Education (CLE) programs generally provide printed program materials, which range from one or two page outlines of the topics covered to full length books. Most often, the materials are standard sized softcover pamphlets of 100 to 200 pages. Many programs are also audio or video taped. Tapes and printed materials may be sold separately. The quality and usefulness of programs vary widely, although they are most useful for practice tips and information about recent developments in statutory and case law. One of the largest and oldest CLE provider in California (and consequently the most prolific supplier of program materials) is CEB (see §10.3). Some national CLE providers produce California-specific materials. The Practicing Law Institute (PLI) and the National Business Institute (NBI) are examples.

§10.11   SELF-HELP BOOKS

Many legal how-to books are directed at the general public. Among the best are those published by Nolo Press. These tend to be written in plain English, and are often California-specific. Nolo's California titles include the following:

Barbara Kaufman's Consumer Action Guide (California edition); softcover; one volume

California Marriage and Divorce Law (11th edition); softcover; one volume

The California Nonprofit Corporation Handbook (6th edition); softcover; one volume; forms on disk

The California Professional Corporation Handbook (4th edition); softcover; one volume

Collect Your Court Judgment (2d California edition); softcover; one volume

The Conservatorship Book (California edition); softcover; one volume

The Criminal Records Book (3d California edition); softcover; one volume

The Deeds Book: How to Transfer Title to Real Property (California edition); softcover; one volume

Everybody's Guide to Municipal Court (California edition); softcover; one volume

Everybody's Guide to Small Claims Court (10th California edition); softcover; one volume

Fight Your Ticket (5th California edition); 1992; softcover; one volume

For Sale by Owner (2d California edition); softcover; one volume

The Guardianship Book (California edition); softcover; one volume

Homestead Your House (8th California edition); softcover; one volume

How to Adopt Your Stepchild in California (3d edition); softcover; one volume

How to Buy a House in California (2d California edition); 1992; softcover; one volume

How to Change Your Name (5th California edition); softcover; one volume

How to Form Your Own California Corporation (7th edition); softcover; one volume

How to Probate an Estate (6th California edition); softcover; one volume

The Landlord's Law Book (3d California edition); softcover; two volumes (Volume 1: Rights and Responsibilities; Volume 2: Evictions)

Nolo's Pocket Guide to California Law; 1992; softcover; one volume

Tenants' Rights (11th California edition); softcover; one volume

CHAPTER 11

VERIFYING AND UPDATING INFORMATION

This chapter outlines the procedure for finding current information, explains the mechanism for verifying the validity of authorities, and introduces Shepard's citations.

§11.1	Finding Current Information	196
§11.2	Verifying Legal Authorities	197
§11.3	Shepard's Citations	198
§11.4	California Authorities in Shepard's	200
§11.5	National Authorities in Shepard's	202

---

§11.1   FINDING CURRENT INFORMATION

Keeping up with new developments is critical in legal research because both the law and the sources that report and analyze it are continually evolving. While various kinds of primary and secondary authority and finding tools are issued and updated differently, the following patterns are common:

Cases. Court opinions are issued as slip opinions on the day of decision and are available from the court at that time, either in print or via the court's electronic bulletin board. Within a day or two, opinions are published in legal newspapers and added to online data bases. Within a few weeks they are published with headnotes and other editorial enhancements in advance sheets, and periodically are added to CD-ROM databases. Eventually, the softcover advance sheets are cumulated into hardcover volumes. The headnotes are topically arranged in digests, which are kept up to date with supplements and with classification tables in the advance sheets.

> Rules of thumb: Check advance sheets, supplements, newspapers, newsletters, and online databases.

Statutes. Pending legislation is reported in legislative documents, newspapers, newsletters, looseleaf services, and online bill tracking databases. Legislative enactments are available from the legislature in a slip format, then cumulated chronologically in softcover advance legislative services, and finally published in official session laws. They are published in their codified format in annotated and unannotated codes, in new or revised volumes or in supplements. They are also available electronically via online databases and CD-ROMs.

> Rules of thumb: Check pocket parts, advance legislative services, and online databases. Call a member of the legislature.

Regulations. Administrative regulations are previewed in newsletters and reported chronologically in official registers. Periodically, they are added to codes of regulations in pamphlet or looseleaf format.

Rules of thumb: Check newsletters and administrative registers. Call the agency issuing the regulations.

Court Rules and Official Forms. These rules and forms are issued by judicial entities and are available from the court clerk. They are announced in the advance sheets and published with periodic updates or replacement volumes in rule services and forms manuals.

Rules of thumb: Check supplements and updates. Call the clerk of the court.

Commentary and Practice Works. Treatises, practice works, and form books are generally either (1) hardcover volumes updated with annual softcover supplements, or (2) looseleaf services updated periodically with new or replacement pages or pamphlets. Newsletters and law reviews are often published monthly or quarterly.

Rules of thumb: Check pocket parts, other print supplements, online databases, and CD-ROM updates. Call the publisher. For current topics, check newspapers, newsletters, and other periodicals.

§11.2   VERIFYING LEGAL AUTHORITIES

Case Law. Two components are involved in verifying case authority:

(1) Direct Validation: Subsequent History of That Case. A case is not good law until (a) it is final in the court of decision, and (b) the time for appeal to a higher court has expired. An additional complication in California is the possibility that the case may be depublished. (On depublication, see §5.10.) The subsequent history of cases is available in Shepard's (see §11.3) and in the online verification services: (1) autocite (on Lexis), and (2) instacite (on Westlaw). In California, cases not yet published in the bound volume of the official reports (i.e., cases in the advance pamphlets) should be verified in the subsequent history table (see §5.12).

(2) <u>Indirect Validation: Treatment of That Case by Later Authorities</u>. The continuing validity of a case as a precedent (see §5.1) depends upon the case being followed by later authorities. A case followed by later cases is strengthened as an authority, while one distinguished or criticized is weakened. An earlier case may also be overruled by a later case or nullified by a later statute. The later treatment of cases is available in Shepard's (see §11.3) and in part in the online verification services: (a) autocite (on Lexis), and (b) instacite (on Westlaw).

<u>Statutory Law</u>. Statutes are verified by Shepardizing (see §11.3), by checking the annotated codes for annotations and recent amendments, and by checking the advance legislative services for treatment during the current session of the legislature. (On advance legislative services, see §6.12.)

<u>Administrative Law</u>. Administrative regulations are verified by Shepardizing (see §11.3), by checking the latest administrative code for the current text, and by checking administrative registers for recent treatment. (On administrative codes and registers, see §8.13 et seq.)

§11.3   SHEPARD'S CITATIONS

Shepard's/McGraw Hill publishes many separate volumes and sets which serve as citators. They provide a mechanism to evaluate the continuing legal validity of an authority by examining subsequent authorities. The idea of Shepard's is to list references to an authority (the "cited" authority) in later authorities (the "citing" authority). For example, a case decided in 1975 may be followed, distinguished, criticized, or overruled in deciding a case in 1980. When the 1975 case is "Shepardized" (looked up in Shepard's), Shepard's will identify the 1980 case for the researcher. A statute or rule may be applied or rejected in deciding a case. Shepardizing the statute or rule will identify the case.

There are Shepard's volumes for the cases, constitutions, statutes, and rules of each state and of the federal system. Shepard's volumes are also available for the Code of Federal

Regulations, the Restatements, and selected law reviews. (On the Code of Federal Regulations, see §8.14; on the Restatements, see §5.23.) Shepard's has a number of topical volumes as well, for example, tax citations, bankruptcy citations, labor cases. Shepard's also publishes case name citators (by plaintiff and defendant) and popular name tables. (On popular name tables, see §11.5.)

Shepard's volumes are arranged by citation of the cited authority. Thus, for example, a California supreme Court case can be shepardized under the California Reports citation, the California Reporter citation, and the Pacific Reporter citation. Shepard's volumes can be difficult for the uninitiated to use, primarily because the scope varies from volume to volume and the numbering and abbreviations are often cryptic. Letters preceding a citation indicate subsequent history and treatment of an authority, superior numbers indicate headnotes in the cited case, and parentheses indicate parallel citations. Each Shepard's volume includes: (1) a list of citations included in the volume, (2) an illustrative case, and (3) table of abbreviations (of reporters cited and of analysis of authority, e.g., o = overruled). In addition, Shepard's publishes an explanatory booklet: How to Shepardize.

Shepard's volumes are kept up to date with a variety of publications, including: (1) hardcover supplements, (2) softcover annual supplements (gold), (3) softcover periodic pamphlets (white), and (4) softcover advance sheets (red). The bound volumes of Shepard's are not cumulative. Softcover pamphlets may or may not be cumulative. If a pamphlet is cumulative (and thus replaces a previous pamphlet), the replacement states on the cover what is to be discarded. Because volumes are not generally cumulative, it may be necessary to look in three or four volumes to completely Shepardize a cited authority.

Generally, cases and statutes are treated in separate volumes of Shepard's, called Case Edition and Statute Edition and are kept up to date with separate softcover pamphlets. Shepard's softcover pamphlets list on the cover "What Your Library Should Contain." Cases are in Part 1, Statutes in Part 2. This is not to be confused with the individual volumes which are also called "part."

§11.4   CALIFORNIA AUTHORITIES IN SHEPARD'S

Shepard's California Citations - Cases; ninth edition; 1992; nine hardcover volumes (maroon). These nine parts of the case edition show citations to California cases as follows:

(1)   Supreme Court Reports, volumes 1-199

(2)   Supreme Court Reports, volumes 200-220; Supreme Court Reports, Second Series; Supreme Court Reports, Third Series, volumes 1-29

(3)   Supreme Court Reports, Third Series, volumes 30-53; miscellaneous reports (including executive agencies and Attorney General opinions); California Appellate Reports, volumes 1-60

(4)   California Appellate Reports, volumes 61-140; California Appellate Reports, Second Series, volumes 1-219

(5)   California Appellate Reports, Second Series, volumes 220-276; California Appellate Reports, Third Series; California Reporter, volumes 1-35

(6)   California Reporter, volumes 36-219

(7)   California Reporter, volumes 220-283; Pacific Reporter, volumes 1-235 (California cases)

(8)   Pacific Reporter, volumes 236-300; Pacific Reporter, Second Series, volumes 1-240 (California cases)

(9)   Pacific Reporter, Second Series, volumes 241-823 (California cases)

The case edition is supplemented by the following:

(1)   Cumulative Supplement, annual softcover pamphlet (gold)

(2)   Quarterly pamphlets (white) and monthly advance sheets (red)

Shepard's California Citations - Statutes; eighth edition; 1988; six hardcover volumes (maroon). These six parts of the statutes edition show citations to California statutes and ordinances as follows:

(1)   United States Constitution and statutes; United States treaties and other international agreements; federal court rules; California Constitution; codes

(2)   Codes

(3) Codes
(4) Codes
(5) Codes; California Administrative Code; orders of the Railroad Commission and the Public Utilities Commission; court rules; jury instructions; includes a Table of California Acts by Popular Names or Short Titles
(6) Uncodified statutes; ordinances; includes an index to charters and an index to ordinances

Note: In Parts 1 through 5, the codes are not always in alphabetical order, e.g., Penal Code is in Part 3 and Government Code is in Part 4.

The statute edition is supplemented by the following:

(1) Statute Edition Supplement, 1988-1990, one hardcover volume (maroon)
(2) Cumulative Supplement, annual softcover pamphlet (gold)
(3) Quarterly pamphlets (white) and monthly advance sheets (red)

Shepard's California Reporter Citations; second edition; 1989; two hardcover volumes (maroon). Part 1 incudes California Reporter volume 1-95. Part 2 includes California Reporter Volumes 96-244. It is supplemented by a Cumulative Supplement - annual softcover (gold), and additional white and red pamphlets.

Shepard's California Citations: CD-ROM Edition

Shepard's California Case Names Citator; first edition; 1985; two hardcover volumes (maroon). This set contains an alphabetical table of cases and citations to California cases from 1950 to date, listed by both plaintiff and defendant. It is supplemented by a Cumulative Supplement and an annual softcover pamphlet (white).

A recent addition to the Shepard's citation system is California Express Citations, which compiles citations to California cases and statutes appearing in recent California cases and federal appellate cases from California. The service includes citing cases appearing in the California Daily Opinion Service, the Daily Appellate Report, and United States Law Week. The publication purports to contain citations not yet available in Shepard's California citations or through computerized research systems.   Express citations are issued biweekly in a softcover (blue) pamphlet and are cumulative.   The service includes:

    (1)   A table of parallel citations
    (2)   A table of depublished cases
    (3)   Citations summaries - a textural discussion of selected, significant citations

§11.5   **NATIONAL AUTHORITIES IN SHEPARD'S**

       Shepard's has volumes for each state, for West's national reporter system (see §5.15), and for federal authorities.   The following additional elements of Shepard's are also useful in various areas of legal research:

Shepard's Law Review Citations; 1986; hardcover (maroon); two volumes; hardcover supplement (1986-1990).

Shepard's Acts and Cases by Popular Name, Federal and State; 1986; hardcover (maroon); two volumes.

Shepard's Restatement of the Law Citations; 1986; hardcover (maroon); one volume.

Shepard's United States Supreme Court Case Name Citator; 1987; hardcover (maroon); one volume.

Shepard's Federal Case Name Citator -- Ninth Circuit Cases; 1987; hardcover (maroon); one volume.

Shepard's Citations for Annotations; 1989; hardcover (maroon); one volume

Shepard's Citations for ALR; 1989; hardcover (maroon); two volumes; shows where annotations are cited in federal and state cases and identifies by citation cases cited in ALR.

Shepard's case citations are available on-line on both Lexis and Westlaw.   Federal tax case citations are also available on CCH Access.

CHAPTER 12

COMPUTERIZED RESEARCH

This chapter introduces the basic components of computer assisted legal research and illustrates products and information available in electronic form.

§12.1   In General   204
§12.2   Software   205
§12.3   Online Databases   207
§12.4   Dialog   209
§12.5   Lexis   210
§12.6   Westlaw   213
§12.7   Periodicals and Periodical Indexes   216
§12.8   CD-ROM   217
§12.9   California CD-ROM Products   217
§12.10   National CD-ROM Products   219

------

§12.1   IN GENERAL

Computers are widely used in law libraries, law firms, corporate legal departments, and government offices. Word processing is effectively universal, and many firms use computers for billing, accounting, payroll, timekeeping, and other facets of law practice management. Software is also available in many areas of practice, including docketing, litigation support, estate planning, trust accounting, tax, and real property. There are numerous document assembly and cite checking programs.

Computer assisted legal research (CALR) involves access to databases, either through software (see §12.2), online services (see §12.3), or compact discs (see §12.8).

Databases tend to be of four types: (1) full text databases, which reproduce the text of selected documents or books, (2) bibliographic databases, which index documents or provide bibliographic information about research sources, (3) directories, and (4) numeric data. Many databases, of course, include elements from more than one of these categories.

Where a print publication is available in a database, the computerized version may not include all that is available in print. For example, a number of periodicals available on line include only substantive articles, comments, and case notes for which authors provide copyright release. In addition, photographs, illustrations, charts, graphs, and page lay-out are rarely preserved.

Interactive video is a teaching tool that combines computer software and a video display. Programs simulate courtroom and practice situations, offer the user choices, and provide immediate feedback. As an example, a user can learn and practice evidentiary objections during simulated testimony. A number of vendors provide interactive videos. In California, CEB (see §10.3) offers a variety of programs under the general title LawQuest.

§12.2   SOFTWARE

Many publishers provide computer software, either as a separate product or as an add-on to existing print products. The Lawyer's PC, a newsletter, includes an annual directory of legal software, and many bibliographic guides to legal publications list software. The American Bar Association Section on Law Practice Management publishes an annual softcover guide to law office computer software vendors, called Locate. The following are illustrative of California products:

Bancroft Whitney; California Civil Practice; forms on disk

Martin Dean's Essential Forms; Judicial Council Forms

Nolo Press; California Incorporator

CCH; Guidebook to California Taxes

Legal Solutions; Judicial Council Forms Preparation Software; federal and county-specific forms also available

Shepard's

    (1)   California Estate Tax Returns: Calculations and Preparation, used in conjunction with companion federal tax software

    (2)   California Fiduciary Income Tax Returns: Calculations and Preparation, used in conjunction with companion federal tax software

    (3)   Lawscribe - California Construction Law (case management system)

Rutter Group

    (1)   Supportax (tax consequences of support obligations; Rule 1274)

    (2)   Community Property Divider

    (3)   California Practice Guide, Alternative Dispute Resolution; forms on disk

Attorney's Brief Case; research software; summaries of cases; full test of some statutes, rules, and regulations

> California Civil Procedure After Trial
> California Civil Procedure Before Trial
> California Criminal Procedure: Charging Through Pretrial
> California Criminal Procedure: Rights of the Accused
> California Evidence: Civil and Criminal
> California Family Law
> Children and the Law

CEB; the following print publications provide forms on disk:

> Advising California Condominium and Homeowners
>   Associations
> Advising California Partnerships
> Business Buy-Sell Agreements
> California Business Practice Forms Manual
> California Civil Procedure Before Trial
> California Durable Power of Attorney Handbook
> California Eviction Defense Manual
> California Marital Termination Agreements
> California Real Property Practice Forms Manual
> California Will Drafting
> Commercial Real Property Lease Practice
> Drafting Agreements for the Sale of Businesses
> Fee Agreement Forms Manual
> Managing an Estate Planning Practice
> Organizing Corporations in California
> Sales and Leases in California Commercial Law Practice
> Judicial Council Forms Manual (Smartlaser II)

Matthew Bender; Draft Master Software (menu-driven document assembly programs) includes:

> California Business Incorporations
> California Depositions and Discovery
> California Durable Powers of Attorney
> California Inter Vivos Trusts
> California Marital Settlement Agreement
> California Personal Injury
> California Simple Wills and Testamentary Trusts

Matthew Bender; CAPS Practice System includes:

> California Forms of Jury Instructions
> California Probate Practice
> California Wills and Trusts

Matthew Bender; TaxCalibre Tax preparation Software (module for California state income tax)

West

> BAJI Forms on Disk
> CALJIC Forms on Disk
> California Judicial Council Forms - Family Law
> California Judicial Council Forms - General Litigation
> California Judicial Council Forms - Probate
> California Civil Code Compact\Fast
> California Code of Civil Procedure Compact\Fast
> California Commercial Code Compact\Fast
> California Corporations Code Compact\Fast
> California Evidence Code Compact\Fast
> California Probate Code Compact\Fast
> California Penal Code Compact\Fast
> California Juvenile Law and Court Rules Compact\Fast
> California Family Law and Rules Compact\Fast
> California Rules of Court, State\Fast
> California Rules of Court, Federal\Fast
> California Secured Transactions Forms\Fast
> California Litigation Practice Forms\Fast

§12.3   ONLINE DATABASES

Many databases are available online. (See Directory of Online Databases; Gale [(313) 961-2242].) The biggest and most widely used distributors of databases in legal research are Westlaw (see §12.6) and Lexis (see §12.5). One of the largest provider of general databases is Dialog (see §12.4). Others of use to lawyers include Vu-Text, Dow Jones News/Retrieval, BRS and ORBIT. Many databases are available from more than one provider. Some illustrative databases include the following:

StateNet; legislative and regulatory reporting service, state and federal; text of federal and California bills, bill status, committee hearings, voting records, campaign contributions, and many other features; (916) 444-0840; also available on Lexis and Westlaw

Legi-Slate; full text and numeric database: Congressional bill, vote and tracking system from 1978

Legi-Tech; full text, numeric and referral database from 1979; legislative history - U.S., California

Electronic Legislative Search System (ELSS); from CCH; referral database - Bill tracking system for Congress and state legislatures

Dow Jones News/Retrieval; market and industry statistics; company profiles; full-text of financial newspapers

OCLC (Online Computer Library Center); EPIC service; electronic catalog of libraries worldwide, arranged by author, title and subject; gateway for many databases from Dialog, BRS, and other providers, including the Index to Legal Periodicals

BNA California Case Law Daily; from BNA; textural database from 1988; summary, analysis and reports of state and federal cases; available on Lexis; Westlaw; Human Resource Information Network

BriefCase OnCall; from Attorney's BriefCase; California, Ninth Circuit and U.S. Supreme Court decisions; indexed by topic, citation, and date; (800) 648-2618; (510) 814-7104; (510) 836-2743

CIS/Index; from Congressional Information Service; bibliographic database from 1988; US Congressional hearings, committee prints, reports and documents; available on Dialog; Orbit Search Service

US Law Week; from BNA; full text database from 1982; available from Lexis; Westlaw; Human Resources Information Network

Prentice Hall Online; public records service available online or without a computer from Prentice Hall [(800) 331-0431]; includes corporate records, UCC filings, bankruptcy, civil judgments, environmental records, tax liens, default notices, civil index, and California real estate data

Trial Line; from Amicus Information Services; civil trial information from California state and federal courts; verdicts; settlements; experts; courts and judges information

Disclosure; (800) 945-3647; national and international public company information, including SEC documents, securities registrations and prospectuses; financial and marketing data

OSHA-FAST; from Fast Codes [(310) 657-9111]; Title 8 of California Code of Regulations (Industrial Relations)

§12.4   DIALOG

Dialog Information Services is one of the largest vendors of databases covering business, medical, social, and scientific topics; both bibliographic and full-text databases, including full text of many magazines, journals, and newspapers. Some Dialog databases are also available on Westlaw (see §12.6). The following databases on dialog are illustrative of those of particular interest to legal researchers:

CIS; from Congressional Information Service; Index to Publications of the United States Congress

Congressional Records Abstracts and Federal Register Abstracts; from National Standards Association

Corporate Affiliations; from National Register Publishing Company

Dialog Company Name Finder, Dialog Journal Name Finder, and Dialog Product Name Finder; from Dialog Information Services

Federal Register; from U.S. Government Printing Office

GPO Monthly Catalog and GPO Publications Reference File; from U.S. Government Printing Office

Trademarkscan - Federal, Trademarkscan - State, and Trademarkscan - UK; from Thomson & Thomson

§12.5   LEXIS

In the Lexis system, the basic unit of information is a document. Documents are combined into files and files into libraries. A single document may appear in a variety of files and libraries. One of the Lexis libraries (CAL) is devoted to California material. It consists of the following files:

Cases:

    CAL = California Supreme Court decisions (1883-date)
    APP = California Court of Appeal and Superior Court Appellate
        Department decisions (1944-date); depublished cases
        (1977-date)

Constitutions and Statutes:

    CODE = Deering's California Codes Annotated - statutes
    CONST = Deering's California Codes Annotated - California
        Constitution
    ALS = Deering's California Codes Annotated - Advance
        Legislative Service
    CATRCK = Tracking pending bills
    CATEXT = Full text of pending bills

    Note: the Table of Contents feature in the CODES library
    provides condensed and detailed outlines of state and federal
    codes

Court Rules:

    RULES = Deering's California Codes Annotates - Rules

Agencies and Regulations:

CAADMN = California Code of Regulations
AG = California Attorney General Opinions (1977-date)
CALSBE = California State Board of Equalization decisions
        (1930-date)
CALSEC = California Department of Corporations opinions
        (1969-date)
CAENV = Water Resources Control Board decisions and decisions
        of predecessor agencies (1924-1990)
CALFTB = California Franchise Tax Board rulings (1953-date)
CAPUC = California Public Utilities Commission decisions
        (1969-date)
CAINC = California Secretary of State corporate information
CALTP = California Secretary of State limited partnership
        information
CAUCC = California Uniform Commercial Code filings
CACON = Contractor License information
CASALE = Sales and use tax permit holder information

County Records:

CAPROP = County Tax Assessor Records
CAPTRF = County Property Transfer Records
RECRDR = San Francisco County Recorder
CALACR = Los Angeles County Criminal Index
CALACV = Los Angeles County Civil Index
CALDBA = Los Angeles County DBA names
CAORCR = Orange County Criminal Index
CAORCV = Orange County Civil Index
CAODBA = Orange County DBA names
CASDCV = San Diego County Civil Index
CASDBA = San Diego County DBA names
CAVDBA = Ventura County DBA names

Treatises:

WITSUM = Witkin, Summary of California Law (9th)
WITPRO = Witkin, California Procedure (3d)
WITEVD = Witkin, California Evidence (3d)
WITCRM = Witkin, California Criminal Law (2d)
WITKIN = Combined Witkin Library

Law Reviews:

        CALLR = California Law Review
        HASTLJ = Hastings Law Journal
        STANLR = Stanford Law Review
        SOCALR = Southern California Law Review
        COMLAW = UCLA Federal Communications Law Journal
        UCLALR = UCLA Law Review

Group Files:

        CASES = CAL, APP, CALSBE, CALFTB, CAPUC, CANEV and CALSEC
        CALTAX = CALSBE and CALFTB
        AGCASE = AG, CAL, APP, CALSBE, CALFTB, CAPUC, CAENV and CALSEC
        CACODE = CODE, CONST, RULES and ALS
        CASOS = CAINC and CALTP
        CABILL = CATRCK and CATEXT

The GUIDE file in the CAL library summarizes the content of each file. It should be checked regularly, since the content of various LEXIS files changes frequently.

The following files (among others) in other Lexis libraries also include California material:

ASSETS library (ALLOWN file) = Local tax assessment and deed transfer records; (CASALE files) = recent deed transfers; (CAPROP file) = California tax assessments and deed transfer records

BNA library (BNACED file) = California Environmental Daily (BNA)

DOCKET library (CABKRT file) = California bankruptcy petitions

ESTATE library (CAL file) = California estate cases

EMPLOY library (CAPER file) = California Public Employee Reporter; (CAL File) = California state employment law cases

LIENS library (CATXLN file) = California federal and state tax liens

FAMILY library (CAL file) = California family law cases

HEALTH library (CAL file) = California health law cases

INCORP library (CABIZ file) = California business information from Secretary of State, Contractors State License Board, selected fictitious business name filings, sales and use tax data

INSLRW library (CAL file) = California insurance law

MEDMAL library (CAL file) = California medical malpractice cases

PRLIAB library (CAL file) = California products liability cases

REALTY library (CAL file) = California real estate cases

STTAX library (CAL file) = California state tax cases

TRADE library (CAL file) = California trade cases

UTILTY library (CAL file) = California public utilities law

VERDCT library (ATLA file) = Verdict and settlement information

§12.6   WESTLAW

Westlaw is an on-line computer assisted legal research system with an extensive database of primary and secondary legal materials, including texts, periodicals, and Shepard's. It allows users to search for documents by citation or by topic, using either the traditional terms and connectors method or, for cases, a new natural language method. Westlaw libraries of California material include the following:

Cases:

>CA-CS = California Supreme Court decisions (1883-date); California Court of Appeal and Superior Court appellate department decisions 1945-date); State Bar Court opinions (1990-date)

Constitutions and Statutes:

>CA-ST = Unannotated statutes
>CA-ST-AN = Annotated statutes
>CA-ST-IDX = Statutes general index
>CA-LEGIS = Legislative service
>CA-BILLS - Full text of pending California bills
>CA-BILLTRK - StateNet bill tracking

Court Rules and Orders:

>CA-Rules = Court rules
>CA-Orders = Court orders

Agencies and Regulations:

>CA-ADC = Barclays Official California Code of Regulations
>CA-ADR = Barclays California Regulatory Code Supplement
>CA-REGTRK = StateNet regulation tracking
>CA-AG = Attorney General opinions (1977-date)
>CAENV-ADMIN = Environmental Law decisions (1982-date)
>CASEC-ADMIN = Securities decisions (1968-date)
>CATX-ADMIN = Taxation decisions (1930-date)
>CATX-ADG = Taxation guidance (1985-date)
>FEHC = Fair Employment and Housing Commission (1978-date)

Newspapers:

>DNLA = Daily News of Los Angeles (1989-date)
>LATIMES = Los Angeles Times (1985-date)
>SCRMTO-BEE = Sacramento Bee (1988-date)
>SF-CHRON = San Francisco Chronicle (1988-date)
>SJMERCURY = San Jose Mercury News (1985-date)

Law Reviews:

BEVHBAJ = Beverly Hills Bar Association Journal (1991-date)
CALR = California Law Review (1985-date)
CALAW = California Lawyer (1984-date)
CAWILJ = California Western International Law Journal
        (1987-date)
CAWLR = California Western Law Review
COMENT = COMM/ENT, Hastings Communications and Entertainment
        Law Journal (1982-date)
ECGLQ = Ecology Law Quarterly (1984-date)
FCLJ = Federal Communications Law Journal (1983-date)
GGULR = Golden Gate University Law Review (1983-date)
HSTCLQ = Hastings Constitutional Law Quarterly (1983-date)
HSTICLR = Hastings International and Comparative Law Review
        (1983-date)
HSTLJ = Hastings Law Journal (1982-date)
HTLJ = High Technology Law Review (1986-date)
INDRELLJ = Industrial Relations Law Journal (1984-date)
INTXBL = International Tax and Business Lawyer (1983-date)
LYLAICLJ = Loyola of Los Angeles International and Comparative
        Law Journal (1990-date)
LYLALR = Loyola of Los Angeles Law Review ((1983-date)
PACLJ = Pacific Law Journal (1983-date)
PEPLR = Pepperdine Law Review (1982 - date)
SANDLR = San Diego Law Review (1983-date)
SCCHITLJ = Santa Clara Computer and High Technology Law
        Journal (1988-date)
SANCLR = Santa Clara Law Review (1982-date)
SCALR = Southern California Law Review (1987-date)
SWULR = Southwestern University Law Review (1983-date)
STENVLJ = Stanford Environmental Law Journal (1987-date)
STJIL = Stanford Journal of International Law (1982-date)
STNLR = Stanford Law Review (1984-date)
TRNATLAW = Transnational Lawyer (1988-date)
UCLALR = UCLA Law Review (1987-date)
UCDLR = University of California at Davis Law Review
        (1983-date)
USFMLJ = University of San Francisco Maritime Law Journal
        (1989-date)
USFLR = University of San Francisco Law Review (1983-date)
WTLR = Whittier Law Review (1983-date)

Other Databases:

     CALS-EO = California State Bar ethics opinions (1977-date)
     BNA-CED = BNA California Environmental Daily (1991-date)
     CA-INSUR = INSURLAW (NILS insurance materials)
     CA-PUR = Public utilities reports
     CA-BAJI = Jury instructions - civil
     CA-CALJIC = Jury instructions - criminal
     CA-JI = BAJI and CALJIC
     CAPRI-WLD = West's Legal Directory - California private
          practice
     ULA = Uniform Laws Annotated
     CCH Standard Federal Tax Reporter

§12.7   PERIODICALS AND PERIODICAL INDEXES

     Many periodicals and periodical indexes are available online,
including the following:

     Index to Legal Periodicals; from H.W. Wilson; bibliographic
     database from 1981; available on Wilsonline; Lexis; Westlaw;
     OCLC Epic. On Lexis, use LAWREV and LEXREF libraries (ILP
     file).

     Legal Resource Index; from Information Access Company;
     bibliographic database from 1980; available on BRS; Dialog;
     Lexis; Westlaw. On Lexis, use LAWREV and LEXREF libraries
     (LGLIND file).

     Criminal Justice Periodicals Index (CJPI); from University
     Microfilms International (UMI); available on Dialog;
     bibliographic database from 1975

     For California law reviews available online see Lexis (§12.5)
and Westlaw (§12.6).

§12.8   CD-ROM

Many legal publishers are experimenting with CD-ROM (compact disc - read only memory) products. Information stored on compact discs is called up on a computer terminal via a CD-ROM drive. Generally, material can be searched in much the same way as online databases, but without charges for online time. Frequently, material can be printed or downloaded to a wordprocessing system.

There are a number of CD directories, providing information about publisher, price, subject matter, coverage, and computer specifications. These include the following:

Directory of Law-Related CD-ROMs; Infosources Publishing [(201) 836-7072]; 1993; indexes by publisher, topic, and search software; quarterly newsletter (Law Related CD-ROM Update).

The CD-ROM Directory, 1992 (7th edition); softcover; UniDisc [(408) 464-0707].

CD-ROMs in Print, annual; Meckler Publishing [(203) 226-6967].

Directory of Portable Databases; semi-annual; Gale [(313) 961-2242].

§12.9   CALIFORNIA CD-ROM PRODUCTS

The following California products are illustrative of those available in a CD-ROM format:

Law Desk (Bancroft Whitney)

    The Complete Witkin Library

    Deering's California Codes Annotated

    California Official Reports; California Reports 2d, 3d and 4th and California Appellate Reports 2d, 3d and 4th; monthly or quarterly updates

California Code of Regulations (Barclays)

Lawdisc (National Legal Databases) - California civil cases; (800) 533-0159

California Reporter on CD-ROM (West) - California cases since 1960; (800) 255-2549; (800) 937-8529

Shepard's California Citations: CD-ROM Edition; monthly replacement; (800) 525-2474, (719) 481-7623 or 488-3000

Search Master California CD-ROM Library (Matthew Bender) - includes California Supreme Court civil opinions from 1883; Court of Appeal civil opinions from 1944; California codes; California Attorney General opinions from 1991; California compensation cases from 1991; approximately 25 treatises and practice works, including California Forms of Pleading and Practice; California Points and Authorities; California Legal Forms--Transaction Guide; (800) 223-1940

§12.10   NATIONAL CD-ROM PRODUCTS

The following national products are illustrative of those available in a CD-ROM format:

Biography Index (H.W. Wilson)
Business Periodicals Index (H.W. Wilson)
Index to Legal Periodicals (H.W. Wilson)
Social Sciences Index (H.W. Wilson)

CCH Access - A collection of discs including: Standard Federal Tax Reporter; Gift and Estate Tax Reporter; Excise Tax Reporter; Internal Revenue Code; Letter Rulings; Tax Court Opinions; U.S. Tax Cases; BTA Decisions; Internal Revenue Manual; Selected IRS Publications; BNA's Tax Management Portfolios

Congressional Masterfile (CIS = Congressional Information Service) - index to Congressional documents, combining (1) US Congressional Committee Hearings Index, (2) Unpublished US Senate Committee Hearings, (3) US Congressional Committee Prints Index, and (4) US Serials Set Index.

InfoTrac (Information Access Company)

(1) Expanded Academic Index: 1500 scholarly and general interest periodicals
(2) General Business File: index to business publications, profiles of public and private companies, brokerage reports on public companies
(3) General Periodicals Index
(4) Government Publications Index
(5) Health Reference Center: index to professional publications and consumer magazines and newsletters, full text reference books and pamphlets, directory of hotlines and support groups
(6) LegalTrac: Legal Resource Index
(7) National Newspaper Index

Martindale Hubbell Law Directory (Martindale-Hubbell Electronic Publishing); does not include Martindale Hubbell Law Digest; (908) 464-6800

Physician's Desk Reference on CD-ROM (Medical Economics Data, Inc.)

Search Master Business Commercial Library (Matthew Bender)
Search Master Collier's Bankruptcy Library (Matthew Bender)
Search Master Federal Library (Matthew Bender)
Search Master Intellectual Property Library (Matthew Bender)
Search Master Personal Injury Library (Matthew Bender)
Search Master Tax Library (Matthew Bender)

West CD-ROM Bankruptcy Library
West CD-ROM BNA Tax Management Portfolios
West CD-ROM Federal Civil Practice Library
West CD-ROM Federal Securities Library
West CD-ROM Federal Tax library
West CD-ROM Government Contracts Library

U.S. Code on CD-ROM; Superintendent of Documents; (202) 783-3238; full code; popular name table; federal court rules

Supreme Court on Disc [U.S. Supreme Court Opinions, 1990-1991] (HyperLaw; (800) 825-6521)

Federal Appeals on Disc; (HyperLaw; (800) 825-6521)

Congressional Record on CD-ROM (FD Inc)

FDA on CD-ROM (FD Inc)

Treaties and International Agreements Researchers' Archives (Tiara) (Oceana Publications; (914) 693-8100)

CHAPTER 13

RESOURCES IN MAJOR PRACTICE AREAS

This chapter lists basic California legal
resources by major practice area. The
material listed is selective and illustrative.

§13.1   Administrative Law   222
§13.2   Business and Corporate Law   222
§13.3   Civil Litigation and Evidence   224
§13.4   Contracts and Commercial Law   227
§13.5   Criminal Law and Procedure   227
§13.6   Environmental Law, Energy, and Water   229
§13.7   Estate Planning, Trusts, and Probate   231
§13.8   Family and Juvenile Law   232
§13.9   Federal Practice   233
§13.10   Financial Institutions and Insurance   234
§13.11   Intellectual Property   235
§13.12   International Law   235
§13.13   Labor, Employment and Workers'
         Compensation   236
§13.14   Law Practice and Legal Services   238
§13.15   Real and Personal Property;
         Landlord-Tenant   239
§13.16   Taxation   241
§13.17   Torts and Products Liability   242

---

§13.1 ADMINISTRATIVE LAW

State Agencies:

Office of Administrative Law

California State Bar:

Public Law Section

Newsletters:

Public Law News; Public Law Section of State Bar
California Regulatory Law Reporter; Center for Public Interest
Law

Practice Works:

California Administrative Hearing Practice; CEB
California Administrative Mandamus; CEB
Handling Claims Against Government Entities; CEB, Action Guide
California Public Agency Practice; Matthew Bender
California Administrative and Antitrust Law; Butterworth
See Witkin, California Procedure 3d, Attorneys §11

§13.2 BUSINESS AND CORPORATE LAW

Statutes:

Business and Professions Code
Corporations Code

California Code of Regulations:

Title 4, Business Regulations
Title 10, Investment
Title 16, Professional and Vocational Regulations

State Agencies:

Department of Corporations
Department of Consumer Affairs

California State Bar:

Business Law Section

Commentary:

Witkin, Summary of California Law, 9th, Partnership
Witkin, Summary of California Law, 9th, Corporations

Newsletters:

Business Law News; Business Law Section of State Bar
Business Law Bulletin (California Edition); Barclays
California Business Law Practitioner; CEB
California Business Law Reporter; CEB

Practice Works:

California Civil Practice: Business module; Bancroft Whitney
California Forms, Legal and Business; Bancroft Whitney
Advising California Nonprofit Corporations; CEB
Advising California Partnerships; CEB
Attorney's Guide to California Professional Corporations; CEB
Attorney's Guide to Trade Secrets; CEB
Business Buy-Sell Agreements; CEB
California Business Practice Forms Manual; CEB
Competitive Business Practices; CEB
Counseling California Corporations; CEB
Drafting Agreements for the Sale of Businesses; CEB
Financing California Businesses; CEB
Organizing Corporations in California; CEB
Proof in Competitive Business Litigation; CEB
Forming and Operating S Corporations; CEB, Action Guide
California Corporation Laws (Ballantine and Sterling); Matthew
    Bender
California Partnership and Proprietors; Matthew Bender
Practice Under the California Corporate Securities Law;
    Matthew Bender

A Business Guide to California Small Claims Court; Parker
California Practice Guide: Corporations; Rutter
Marsh's California Corporation Law; Prentice Hall
The California Nonprofit Corporation Handbook; Nolo
The California Professional Corporation Handbook; Nolo
How to Form Your Own California Corporation; Nolo
See Witkin, California Procedure 3d, Attorneys §17

§13.3   CIVIL LITIGATION AND EVIDENCE

Statutes:

Code of Civil Procedure
Evidence Code

California State Bar:

Litigation Section

Commentary:

Witkin, California Procedure, 3d
Witkin, California Evidence, 3d
Restatement of Judgments

Newsletters:

Alternative Dispute Resolution Newsalert (California Edition);
    Bancroft Whitney
California Civil Law Reporter (Law Alert); La Jolla Legal
    Publications
California Litigation; Litigation Section of State Bar
Civil Litigation Reporter; CEB

Practice Works:

California Judicial Council Forms Manual; Bancroft Whitney
California Civil Practice: Civil Procedure module; Bancroft
    Whitney
California Trial Handbook; Bancroft Whitney

California Negotiation and Settlement Handbook; Bancroft Whitney
Modern California Discovery; Bancroft Whitney
California Civil Appellate Practice; CEB
California Lis Pendens Practice; CEB
California Civil Litigation Forms Manual; CEB
California Civil Procedure Before Trial; CEB
California Civil Procedure During Trial; CEB
California Civil Writ Practice; CEB
California Evidence Benchbook; CEB
California Judicial Council Forms Manual: CEB
California Trial Objections; CEB
Civil Discovery Practice in California; CEB
Effective Direct and Cross-Examination; CEB
Effective Introduction of Evidence in California; CEB
Jefferson's Synopsis of California Evidence Law; CEB
Persuasive Opening Statements and Closing Arguments; CEB
Practicing California Judicial Arbitration; CEB
Creating Your Discovery Plan; CEB, Action Guide
Enforcing Civil Money Judgments; CEB, Action Guide
Handling Civil Appeals; CEB, Action Guide
Handling Civil Writs in the Courts of Appeal; CEB, Action Guide
Handling Depositions; CEB, Action Guide
Handling Expert Witnesses in California Courts; CEB, Action Guide
Handling Service of Process (Serving Summons in Civil Proceedings); CEB, Action Guide
Handling Subpenas; CEB, Action Guide
Laying a Foundation to Introduce Evidence (Preparing and Using Evidence at Trial); CEB, Action Guide
Making a Summary Judgment Motion; CEB, Action Guide
Moving to Compel Discovery and Other Discovery Motions; CEB, Action Guide
Obtaining Appointment of a Receiver (And Monitoring the Receivership); CEB, Action Guide
Obtaining an Injunction; CEB, Action Guide
Obtaining a Writ of Attachment; CEB, Action Guide
Obtaining Discovery: Initiating and Responding to Discovery Procedures; CEB, Action Guide
Preparing for Trial; CEB, Action Guide
California Civil Actions--Pleading and Practice; Matthew Bender

California Deposition and Discovery Practice; Matthew Bender
California Forms of Pleading and Practice; Matthew Bender
California Trial Guide; Matthew Bender
California Complex Litigation Manual; Parker
California Courtroom Evidence; Parker
California Damages: Law and Proof; Parker
California Objections at Trial; Parker
California Preliminary Examinations; Parker
California Trial Techniques; Parker
Guide to California Evidence; Parker
California Practice Guide: Alternative Dispute Resolution;
    Rutter
California Practice Guide: Civil Appeals and Writs; Rutter
California Practice Guide: Civil Procedure Before Trial;
    Rutter
California Practice Guide: Civil Trials and Evidence; Rutter
California Practice Guide: Enforcing Judgments and Debts;
    Rutter
Appeals Procedure Manual, Association of Municipal Court
    Clerks
Civil Procedure Manual, Association of Municipal Court Clerks
Civil Defaults and Default Judgments Manual, Association of
    Municipal Court Clerks
Small Claims Manual, Association of Municipal Court Clerks
California Judges Benchbook, Small Claims Court and Consumer
    Law; CJER
California ADR Practice Guide; Shepard's
California Arbitration Practice Guide; Lawpress
California Civil Trialbook; West
Collect Your Court Judgment (California edition); Nolo
Everybody's Guide to Municipal Court (California edition);
    Nolo
Everybody's Guide to Small Claims Court (California edition);
    Nolo
See Witkin, California Procedure 3d, Attorneys §§12, 26

§13.4   CONTRACTS AND COMMERCIAL LAW

Statutes:

> Public Contracts Code
> Uniform Commercial Code

State Agencies:

> Department of Consumer Affairs

Commentary:

> Witkin, Summary of California Law, 9th, Contracts
> Witkin, Summary of California Law, 9th, Sales
> Restatement of Contracts

Practice Works:

> California Breach of Contract Remedies; CEB
> California Surety and Fidelity Bond Practice; CEB
> Debt Collection Practice in California; CEB
> Sales and Leases in California Commercial Law Practice; CEB
> Secured Transactions in California Commercial Law Practice; CEB
> Barbara Kaufman's Consumer Action Guide (California edition); Nolo
> See Witkin, California Procedure 3d, Attorneys §15

§13.5   CRIMINAL LAW AND PROCEDURE

Statutes:

> Penal Code

California Code of Regulations:

> Title 15, Crime Prevention and Corrections

State Agencies:

Department of Corrections
Board of Prison Terms
Youth Authority
Youthful Offender Parole Board
Office of Criminal Justice Planning
Prison Industry Authority
State Public Defender

California State Bar:

Criminal Law Section
Certified specialty

Commentary:

Witkin, California Criminal Law, 2d; Bancroft Whitney
Criminal Justice Journal (Western State University)

Newsletters:

California Criminal Defense Practice Reporter; Matthew Bender
California Criminal Law Reporter; La Jolla Legal Publications
Criminal Law News; Criminal Law Section of State Bar
Ninth Circuit Criminal Law Reporter

Practice Works:

California Criminal Forms and Instructions; Bancroft Whitney
Appeals and Writs in Criminal Cases; CEB
California Criminal Law Procedure and Practice; CEB
California Search and Seizure Practice; CEB
Defending Your Client in a Misdemeanor Case (Including a DUI);
    CEB, Action Guide
California Criminal Defense Practice; Matthew Bender
California White Collar Crimes; Parker
Criminal Procedure Manual, Association of Municipal Court
    Clerks
California Judges Benchbook, Criminal Pretrial Proceedings;
    CJER
California Judges Benchbook, Criminal Trials; CJER

California Judges Benchbook, Criminal Posttrial Proceedings;
    CJER
California Judges Benchbook, Search and Seizure; CJER
The Criminal Records Book (California edition); Nolo
Fight Your Ticket (California edition); Nolo
See Witkin, California Procedure 3d, Attorneys §18

§13.6   ENVIRONMENTAL LAW, ENERGY, AND WATER

Statutes:

    Fish and Game Code
    Harbors and Navigation Code
    Public Resources Code
    Public Utilities Code
    Water Code

California Code of Regulations:

    Title 14, Natural Resources
    Title 20, Public Utilities and Energy
    Title 23, Waters
    Title 26, Toxics

State Agencies:

    Air Resources Board
    Integrated Waste Management Board
    Department of Pesticide Regulation
    Water Resources Control Board
    Department of Boating and Waterways
    California Coastal Commission
    State Coastal Conservancy
    California Conservation Corps
    Department of Conservation
    Department of Fish and Game
    Board of Forestry
    Department of Forestry and Fire Protection
    Mining and Geology Board
    Department of Parks and Recreation

Department of Water Resources
Wildlife Conservation Board
California Wildlife Foundation
Energy Commission
Fish and Game Commission
Department of Food and Agriculture
Reclamation Board
Water Commission

Commentary:

Witkin, Summary of California Law, 9th, Real Property
Ecology Law Quarterly (Berkeley)
Journal of Law and Environment (University of Southern
        California)
U.C.L.A. Journal of Environmental Law and Policy
Stanford Environmental Law Journal

Newsletters:

California Environmental Law and Regulation Reporter;
        Shepard's
California Environmental Insider; California Environmental
        Publications
California Water Law and Policy Reporter; Shepard's

Practice Works:

Minimizing Toxics Liability When Buying Real Property and
        Businesses; CEB, Action Guide
California Environmental Law and Land Use Practice; Matthew
        Bender
California Hazardous Waste Management; California
        Environmental Publications
See Witkin, California Procedure 3d, Attorneys §24

§13.7   ESTATE PLANNING, TRUSTS, AND PROBATE

Statutes:

    Probate Code

Judicial Council Forms:

    Decedents' Estates - DE-110 et seq.
    Guardianships and Conservatorships - GC-020 et seq.

California State Bar:

    Estate Planning, Trust & Probate Law Section
    Certified specialty

Commentary:

    Witkin, Summary of California Law, 9th, Trusts
    Witkin, Summary of California Law, 9th, Wills and Probate
    Restatement of Trusts
    Restatement of Property

Newsletters:

    Estate Planning and California Probate Reporter; CEB
    Estate Planning, Trust and Probate News; Estate Planning,
        Trust and Probate Section of State Bar
    Gilfix California Elder Law Newsalert; Bancroft Whitney

Practice Works:

    California Conservatorships and Guardianships; CEB
    Decedent Estate Practice; CEB
    California Durable Power of Attorney Handbook; CEB
    California Elder Law: An Advocate's Guide; CEB
    California Probate Workflow Manual; CEB
    California Trust Administration; CEB
    California Will Drafting; CEB
    Drafting California Irrevocable Living Trusts; CEB
    Drafting California Revocable Living Trusts; CEB
    Estate Planning Practice; CEB

Managing an Estate Planning Practice; CEB
Transferring Property Without Probate; CEB, Action Guide
California Medi-Cal Guide; CCH
California Probate Practice; Matthew Bender
California Wills and Trusts; Matthew Bender
California Probate Procedure; Parker
California Practice Guide: Probate; Rutter
The Conservatorship Book (California edition); Nolo
The Guardianship Book (California edition); Nolo
How to Probate an Estate (California edition); Nolo
See Witkin, California Procedure 3d, Attorneys §23

§13.8   FAMILY AND JUVENILE LAW

Statutes:

Family Code

Rules of Court:

Section 1201 et seq. (Family Law Rules)
Section 1400 et seq. (Juvenile Court Rules)

Judicial Council Forms:

Family Law - General Practice - No. 1281 et seq.
Family Law - Joinder - No. 1291-10 et seq.
Family Law - Discovery - No. 1292.10 et seq.
Family Law - Summary Dissolution - No. 1295.10 et seq.
Family Law - Domestic Violence - No. 1295.90 et seq.
Family Law - Parentage - No. 1986.60 et seq.
Family Law - Expedited child Support - No. 1297 et seq.
Civil Harassment - CH-100 et seq.
Juvenile - JV-100 et seq.

California State Bar:

Family Law Section
Certified specialty

Commentary:

> Witkin, Summary of California Law, 9th, Parent and Child
> Witkin, Summary of California Law, 9th, Husband and Wife
> Witkin, Summary of California Law, 9th, Community Property
> Journal of Juvenile Law (University of LaVerne)

Newsletters:

> California Family Law Report and California Family Law First
> Alert; California Family Law Report, Inc.
> California Family Law Monthly; Matthew Bender
> Family Law News: Family Law Section of State Bar

Practice Works:

> California Juvenile Court Practice; CEB
> California Marital Termination Agreements; CEB
> Practice Under the California Family Law Act: Dissolution,
>   Legal Separation, Nullity; CEB
> Approaching a Marital Dissolution; CEB, Action Guide
> California Community Property with Tax Analysis; Matthew
>   Bender
> California Family Law--Practice and Procedure; Matthew Bender
> California Family Tax Planning; Matthew Bender
> California Community Property Handbook; Parker
> California Practice Guide: Family Law; Rutter
> Basic California Family Law Handbook; California Family Law
>   Report
> California Family Law Practice; California Family Law Report
> California Marriage and Divorce Law; Nolo
> How to Adopt Your Stepchild in California; Nolo
> See Witkin, California Procedure 3d, Attorneys §19

§13.9   FEDERAL PRACTICE

Practice Works:

> Handling a Chapter 7 Consumer Bankruptcy; CEB, Action Guide
> Moving for Relief from an Automatic Stay in Bankruptcy; CEB,
>   Action Guide

Handling Expert Witnesses in Federal Courts; CEB, Action Guide
Removing an Action to Federal Court; CEB, Action Guide
Representing a Debtor in chapter 7 Business Bankruptcy; CEB, Action Guide
California Practice Guide: Federal Civil Procedure Before Trial; Rutter
See Witkin, California Procedure 3d, Attorneys §20

§13.10   FINANCIAL INSTITUTIONS AND INSURANCE

Statutes:

Financial Code
Insurance Code

State Agencies:

Department of Banking
Department of Savings and Loan

Commentary:

Witkin, Summary of California Law, 9th, Negotiable Instruments

Newsletters:

California Insurance Law and Regulation Reporter; Shepard's

Practice Works:

California Automobile Insurance Law Guide; CEB
California Insurance Disputes; Parker
California Insurance Law and Practice; Matthew Bender

§13.11   INTELLECTUAL PROPERTY

California State Bar:

Intellectual Property Section

Commentary:

COMM/ENT (Hastings; Communications and Entertainment)
Federal Communications Law Journal (UCLA)
High Technology Law Journal (Berkeley)
Santa Clara Computer and High Technology Law Journal

Newsletters:

New Matter; Intellectual Property Section of State Bar

Practice Works:

California Intellectual Property Handbook; Matthew Bender

§13.12   INTERNATIONAL LAW

State Agencies:

Office of California-Mexican Affairs
Office of International Affairs

California State Bar:

International Law Section

Commentary:

California Western International Law Journal
Hastings International and Comparative Law Review
International Tax and Business Lawyer (Berkeley)
Stanford Journal of International Law

Loyola of Los Angeles International and Comparative Law
    Journal
Transnational Lawyer (University of the Pacific)
Restatement of Foreign Relations Law of the United States

Newsletters:

International Practitioner; International Law Section of State
    Bar

Directories:

Foreign Government Offices in California: A Directory;
    California Institute of Public Affairs

§13.13   LABOR, EMPLOYMENT, AND WORKERS' COMPENSATION

Statutes:

Labor Code
Unemployment Insurance Code

California Code of Regulations:

Title 8, Industrial Relations

State Agencies:

    Department of Fair Employment and Housing
    Fair Employment and Housing Commission
    Agricultural Labor Relations Board
    Department of Industrial Relations
    Industrial Welfare Commission
    Public Employment Relations Board
    Unemployment Insurance Appeals Board
    Workers' Compensation Appeals Board

California State Bar:

    Labor & Employment Law Section
    Workers' Compensation Section
    Certified specialty in workers' compensation

Commentary:

    Witkin, Summary of California Law, 9th, Agency and Employment
    Witkin, Summary of California Law, 9th, Workers' Compensation
    Industrial Relations Law Journal (Berkeley)
    Restatement of Agency

Newsletters:

    California Employment Law Reporter; Matthew Bender
    California Labor & Employment; Labor & Employment Section of
        State Bar
    California Labor and Employment Alert for All California
        Employers; Castle Publications
    California Employee Relations Report; BNA
    Labor Law Bulletin (California Edition); Barclays
    Workers' Compensation Quarterly; Workers' Compensation Section
        of State Bar

Practice Works:

    Advising California Employers; CEB
    Attorney's Guide to Pension and Profit-Sharing Plans; CEB
    California Workers' Compensation Practice; CEB
    California Workers' Damages Practice; CEB
    Wrongful Employment Termination Practice; CEB
    Handling a Wrongful Termination Action; CEB, Action Guide
    California Employment Law; Matthew Bender
    California Employers' Guide to Employee Handbooks and
        Personnel Policy Manuals; Matthew Bender
    California Law of Employee Injuries and Worker's Compensation;
        Matthew Bender
    California Public Sector Labor Relations; Matthew Bender
    Workers' Compensation Law of California; Matthew Bender
    California Unemployment and Disability Compensation Programs;
        Parker
    California Unemployment Insurance Handbook; Parker

California Workers' Compensation Claims and Benefits; Parker
California Workers' Compensation Law; Parker
California Workers' Compensation Handbook; Parker
Labor and Employment in California; Parker
See Witkin, California Procedure 3d, Attorneys §§21, 27

§13.14   LAW PRACTICE AND LEGAL SERVICES

California State Bar:

General Practice Section
Law Practice Management Section
Legal Services Section

Commentary:

Witkin, California Procedure, 3d, Attorneys

Newsletters:

The General Practitioner; General Practice Section of State
     Bar
The Bottom Line; Law Practice Management Section of State Bar
Legal Services Section News; Legal Services Section of State
     Bar

Practice Works:

California Attorney's Damages Guide; CEB
California Attorney's Fees Award Practice; CEB
Fee Agreement Forms Manual; CEB
Effectively Handling Your Client Relationship; CEB, Action
     Guide
California Attorney Practice; Matthew Bender
California Practice Guide: Law Practice Management; Rutter

§13.15   REAL AND PERSONAL PROPERTY; LANDLORD-TENANT

California Code of Regulations:

    Title 25, Housing and Community Development

State Agencies:

    Department of Housing and Community Development
    Department of Fair Employment and Housing
    Fair Employment and Housing Commission
    Housing Finance Agency
    Department of Real Estate

California State Bar:

    Real Property Law Section

Commentary:

    Witkin, Summary of California Law, 9th, Secured Transaction in
        Personal Property
    Witkin, Summary of California Law, 9th, Security Transactions
        in Real Property
    Witkin, Summary of California Law, 9th, Personal Property
    Witkin, Summary of California Law, 9th, Real Property
    Restatement of Property

Newsletters:

    California Real Property Journal; Real Property Law Section of
        State Bar
    Miller and Starr California Real Estate Newsalert; Bancroft
        Whitney
    Land Use Forum; CEB
    Real Property Law Reporter; CEB
    California Real Estate Reporter; Matthew Bender
    California Construction Law Reporter; Shepard's
    California Land Use Law and Policy Reporter; Shepard's

Practice Works:

> Miller and Starr California Real Estate; Bancroft Whitney
> California Condominium Handbook; Bancroft Whitney
> Advising California Condominium and Homeowners Associations;
>   CEB
> Attorney's Guide to California Construction Contracts and
>   Disputes; CEB
> California Condominium and Planned Development Practice; CEB
> California Eviction Defense Manual; CEB
> California Mechanics' Liens and Other Remedies; CEB
> California Mortgage and Deed of Trust Practice; CEB
> California Real Property Financing; CEB
> California Real Property Practice Forms Manual; CEB
> California Real Property Remedies Practice; CEB
> California Real Property Sales Transactions; CEB
> California Residential Landlord-Tenant Practice; CEB
> California Subdivision Map Act Practice; CEB
> California Title Insurance Practice; CEB
> California Zoning Practice; CEB
> Commercial Real Property Lease Practice; CEB
> Condemnation Practice in California; CEB
> Ground Lease Practice; CEB
> Guide to California Subdivision Sales Law; CEB
> Landslide and Subsidence Liability; CEB
> Real Property Exchanges; CEB
> Approaching Construction Disputes; CEB, Action Guide
> Enforcing Security Interests in Personal Property; CEB, Action
>   Guide
> Handling a Real Estate Broker Liability Action; CEB, Action
>   Guide
> Handling a Real Property Foreclosure; CEB, Action Guide
> Handling Mechanics' Liens and Related Remedies (Private
>   Works); CEB, Action Guide
> Handling Public Works Remedies: Stop Notices and Payment
>   Bonds; CEB, Action Guide
> Handling Real Property Sales Transactions; CEB, Action Guide
> Handling Unlawful Detainers; CEB, Action Guide
> Making a Claim Under a Title Insurance Policy; CEB, Action
>   Guide
> Obtaining a Writ of Possession; CEB, Action Guide
> Taking Security Interests in Personal Property; CEB, Action
>   Guide

California Mechanics' Lien Law and Construction Industry
    Practice; Matthew Bender
California Real Estate Law and Practice; Matthew Bender
California Mechanics' Lien Law Handbook; Parker
California Foreclosure: Law and Practice; Shepard's
California Land Use Procedure; Shepard's
California Construction Law Manual; Shepard's
California Real Estate Forms and Commentaries; Prentice Hall
The Deeds Book: How to Transfer Title to Real Property
    (California edition); Nolo
For Sale by Owner (California edition); Nolo
Homestead Your House (California edition); Nolo
How to Buy a House in California; Nolo
The Landlord's Law Book (California edition); Nolo
Tenants' Rights (California edition); Nolo
See Witkin, California Procedure 3d, Attorneys §§16, 24

§13.16   TAXATION

Statutes:

Revenue and Taxation Code

State Agencies:

Franchise Tax Board
Board of Equalization

California State Bar:

Taxation Section
Certified specialty

Commentary:

Witkin, Summary of California Law, 9th, Taxation

Newsletters:

California Tax Lawyer; Taxation Section of State Bar

Practice Works:

> California Taxes; CEB
> Personal Tax Planning for Professionals and Owners of Small
>   Businesses; CEB
> Tax Aspects of California Partnerships; CEB
> Tax Aspects of Marital Dissolutions; CEB
> Taxation of Real Property Transfers; CEB
> Tax Practice in California: A Guide to Federal Procedure; CEB
> California Taxation; Matthew Bender
> California Closely Held Corporations: Tax Planning and
>   Practice Guide; Matthew Bender
> California State and Local Taxes; Research Institute of
>   America
> Taxing California Property; Clark Boardman Callaghan
> Guidebook to California taxes; CCH
> California Tax Guide; CCH
> See Witkin, California Procedure 3d, Attorneys §25

§13.17   TORTS AND PRODUCTS LIABILITY

Commentary:

> Witkin, Summary of California Law, 9th, Torts
> Restatement of Torts

Newsletters:

> California Tort Reporter; Shepard's

Practice Works:

> California Civil Practice: Torts module; Bancroft Whitney
> California Personal Injury Digest; Bancroft Whitney
> California Personal Injury Forms; Bancroft Whitney,
> California Drunk Driving Defense; Bancroft Whitney
> Basic Personal Injury Anatomy; CEB
> California Expert Witness Guide; CEB
> California Government Tort Liability Practice; CEB

California Liability Insurance Practice: Claims and
    Litigation; CEB
California Personal Injury Proof; CEB
California Tort Damages; CEB
California Tort Guide; CEB
California Uninsured Motorist Practice; CEB
Debt Collection Tort Practice; CEB
California Products Liability Actions; Matthew Bender
California Torts; Matthew Bender
California Uninsured Motorist Law; Parker
California Practice Guide: Bad Faith; Rutter
California Practice Guide: Personal Injury; Rutter
California Products Liability, Law and Practice; West
See Witkin, California Procedure 3d, Attorneys §22

INDEX

Abbreviations	§1.14
Administrative agencies	
Alphabetical list	§8.4
Guides	§8.2
Opinions and services	§8.12
Structure of executive branch	§8.3
Administrative law	
In general	§8.1 et seq.
Online sources	§§12.5, 12.6
Practice resources	§13.1
Tips for finding	§8.17
Administrative Office of the Courts	§4.11
Advance legislative services	§6.12
Advance report of cases	§5.5
Advance sheets	
Bancroft Whitney	§5.6
In general	§2.16
West	§5.7
ALR	§5.22
American Law Reports	§5.22
Annotation	§§2.8, 5.22
Appellate department of superior court	§§4.9, 5.9
Appellate time deadlines	§5.11
Assembly standing committees	§6.5
Association of Municipal Court Clerks	
Practice works	§10.9
Attorney General Opinions	§8.7
Authority	
Primary and secondary distinguished	§1.2
Mandatory and persuasive distinguished	§1.3
BAJI	§4.23
Bancroft Whitney	
Advance sheets	§5.6
CD-ROM	§12.9
Digests	§5.19
Newsletters	§9.11
Practice works	§10.2
Software	§12.2
Witkin	§9.2
Bankruptcy court	§4.5

Bar associations   §3.6
    ABA sections   §9.6
    Journals   §3.4
    Local associations   §3.5
    National associations   §9.11
    Newsletters   §3.4
    Specialty associations
    See - State Bar of California
Bibliographic sources   §1.11
Bill numbering   §6.8
Binding   §2.9
Brief of case   §5.17
Business law
    Practice resources   §13.2

California
    Code of Regulations   §8.13
    Codes   §7.5
    Constitution   §7.2
    Court of Appeal   §4.8
    Executive branch   §8.3
    Judges Association   §4.16
    Judicial branch   §4.6 et seq.
    Justice Court   §4.10
    Legislative branch   §6.3
    Municipal Court   §4.10
    Session laws   §6.11
    Superior Court   §§4.9, 5.9
    Supreme Court   §4.7
CALJIC   §4.23
Cases
    Advance reports   §5.5
    Briefs   §5.17
    California   §5.4
    Depublication   §5.10
    Federal   §5.14
    In general   §5.2
    Online sources   §§12.5, 12.6
    Reports and reporters   §5.3
    Selective publication   §5.9
    Subsequent history table   §5.12
    Tips for finding   §5.16
    See - Advance sheets
    See - Reports and reporters
CCH   §8.16

CD-ROM
    California titles   §12.9
    In general   §12.8
    National titles   §12.9

CEB
    Action guides   §10.4
    In general   §10.3
    Newsletters   §9.11
    Practice works   §10.5
    Software   §12.2

Center of Judicial Education and Research
    See - CJER

CFR   §8.14
Chapter laws   §6.11
CIS   §6.19
Civil litigation
    Practice resources   §13.3

CJER
    Benchbooks   §10.9
    In general   §4.17

CLE - see Continuing legal education
Citation   §1.15
Citation Guide   §5.13
Civil and criminal distinguished   §1.4
Code of Federal Regulations   §§8.14, 8.15
Codes
    Annotated   §7.6
    California   §7.5
    Electronic form   §7.8
    LARMAC   §7.9
    Numbering   §7.10
    Online sources   §§12.5, 15.6
    Unannotated   §7.7
    United States Code   §7.6
    See - Statutes
Codification   §7.3
Collateral references   §2.7
Commerce Clearing House   §8.16
Commercial law
    Practice resources   §13.4
Commission on Judicial Appointments   §4.14
Commission on Judicial Performance   §4.15
Common law   §5.1
Compact Disc - see CD-ROM
Comparative law   §9.13
Computerized research   §12.1 et seq.
Congressional Index   §6.17
Congressional Information Service   §6.19

Constitutional law   §7.1
Continuing legal education
        In general   §3.9
        Program materials   §10.10
Contract law
        Practice resources   §13.4
Corporate law
        Practice resources   §13.2
Court of Appeal
        California   §4.8
        Federal   §4.5
Courts
        Appellate court structure   §4.3
        Directories   §4.24
        Fees   §4.4
        Opinions - see Cases
        Records   §4.4
        Tier structure   §4.3
        Trial court structure   §4.3
        See - California courts
        See - Federal courts
Criminal and civil distinguished   §1.4
Criminal law
        Practice resources   §13.5
Cross reference   §2.6
Cumulation   §2.17
Current information, tips for finding   §11.1

Databases   §12.3
Deering's Codes   §7.6
Department of Corporations   §8.10
Department of Justice   §8.6
Depublication of cases   §5.10
Deskbooks   §9.14
Dewey decimal classification   §1.9
Dialog   §12.4
Dictionaries   §1.13
Digests
        Bancroft Whitney   §5.19
        Federal   §5.14
        In general   §5.18
        West   §5.19
Directories
        Courts and judges   §4.34
        Lawyers   §3.7

Editions, new and revised   §2.15
Employment law
        Practice resources   §13.13
Encyclopedias   §9.3
Environmental law
        Practice resources   §13.6
Equity and law distinguished   §1.4
Estate planning
        Practice resources   §13.7
Evidence law
        Practice resources   §13.3

Family law
        Practice resources   §13.8
Federal and state law distinguished   §1.4
Federal courts
        Court of Appeal   §4.5
        District Court   §4.5
        Rules and forms   §4.21
        Supreme Court   §4.5
Federal judicial system   §4.5
Federal law
        Practice resources   §13.9
Federal legislative system   §6.2
Federal session laws   §6.7
Filing instructions   §2.18
Financial institutions law
        Practice resources   §13.10
Finding tools   §1.2
Format of research materials   §2.1
Former section   §7.11
Forms
        Federal court   §4.21
        Form books   §10.1 et seq.
        Local court   §4.20
        Judicial Council   §4.18
Franchise Tax Board   §8.8

Indexes
        In general   §2.5
        Statutory   §7.9
Insurance law
        Practice resources   §13.10
Intellectual property law
        Practice resources   §13.11

International law
    Practice resources   §13.12

Jargon   §1.16
Judges
    California Judges Association   §4.16
    Center for Judicial Education
    and Research   §4.17
    Commission on Judicial Appointments   §4.14
    Commission on Judicial Performance   §4.15
    Directories   §4.24
Judicial branch of government   §4.1 et seq.
Judicial Council
    Forms   §4.18
    Organization   §4.11
    Rules of Court   §4.19
Jurisdiction
    Court of Appeal   §4.8
    Concept   §4.2
    Municipal and Justice Courts   §4.10
    Superior Court   §4.9
    Supreme Court   §4.7
Jury instructions   §4.23
Justice Court   §4.10
Juvenile law
    Practice resources   §13.8

Key number system   §5.21

Labor law
    Practice resources   §13.13
Landlord-Tenant law
    Practice resources   §13.15
LARMAC   §7.9
Law and equity distinguished   §1.4
Law practice - see Lawyers
Law Reviews
    California titles   §9.8
    Classification   §9.6
    Indexes   §§9.9, 12.7
    Online sources   §§12.5, 12.6
    Use   §9.7
Law Revision Commission   §4.13

Law schools
    In general   §3.10
    Text books   §9.4
Lawyers
    Continuing legal education   §§3.9, 10.10
    Directories   §3.7
    Ethics   §3.8
    In general   §3.1 et seq.
    Practice resources   §13.14
    Regulation   §3.1
    Specialization   §3.2
    See - State Bar of California
Legal research guides   §1.12
Legal service providers   §1.7
Legislation
    Advance legislative services   §6.12
    Bill numbering   §6.8
    Chapter laws   §6.11
    Effective date in California   §7.12
    Lifecycle   §6.4
    Pending   §6.20
    See - Codes
    See - Statutes
Legislative branch of government   §6.1 et seq.
Legislative history
    In general   §6.13
    Services   §6.14
Legislative publications   §§6.15, 6.16
Lexis   §12.5
Libraries
    In general   §1.8
    Classification systems   §1.9
Library of Congress classification system   §1.9
Litigation and transactions distinguished §1.4
Local court rules and forms   §4.20
Looseleaf
    Format   §2.13
    Services   §8.16

Mandatory authority   §1.3
Matthew Bender
    CD-ROM   §§12.9, 12.10
    Newsletters   §9.11
    Practice works   §10.6
    Software   §12.2
MCLE - see Continuing legal education
Microfiche   §2.19

Multivolume sets   §2.10
Municipal Court   §4.10

Newsletters
    California titles   §9.11
    In general   §9.10
Newspapers
    Advance report of cases   §5.5
    In general   §9.12
    Online sources   §12.6
Nolo Press   §10.11

Online databases   §12.3 et seq.
On point   §1.3
Outline   §2.3

Parallel reference tables   §2.4
Parker practice works   §10.7
Pathfinders   §1.10
Pending legislation   §6.20
Periodicals
    Indexes   §§9.9, 12.7
    In general   §9.5
    See - Law reviews
Personal property law
    Practice resources   §13.15
Persuasive authority   §1.3
Physical characteristics of research tools   §2.1 et seq.
Pocket parts   §2.11
Popular name tables   §§2.4, 7.14
Practice works   §10.1 et seq.
Precedent   §5.1
Primary authority   §1.2
Prior law   §7.11
Probate law
    Practice resources   §13.7
Problem solving   §1.17
Procedure and substance distinguished   §1.4
Products liability law
    Practice resources   §13.17
Propositions, numbering   §7.18
Public Utilities Commission   §8.11
Publishers
    list   §1.5
    catalogs   §1.6

Real property law
    practice resources   §13.15
Regulations
    California   §8.13
    Federal   §§8.14, 8.15
Reporter of Decisions   §4.12
Reports and reporters
    Federal   §5.14
    In general   §5.3
    West reporter system   §5.15
    See - Cases
Replacement volumes   §2.12
Research tips - see Tips
Restatements   §5.23
Revised volumes   §2.14
Rules
    California Rules of Court   §4.19
    Federal court rules   §4.21
    Local court rules   §4.20
    Online sources   §§12.5, 12.6
    Publications   §4.22
    State Bar rules   §3.3
Rutter Group
    Practice works   §10.6
    Software   §12.2

Secondary authority   §1.2
Secretary of State   §8.5
Sections and section numbering   §2.2
Selective publication of cases   §5.9
Self-help books   §10.11
Senate standing committees   §6.6
Series (2d, 3d, 4th)   §2.15
Session laws
    California   §6.11
    Federal   §6.10
Shelving instructions   §2.18
Shepard's
    CD-ROM   §12.9
    Citators   §11.3 et seq.
    Newsletters   §9.11
    Practice works   §10.6
    Software   §12.2
Slip   §§2.2, 5.5
Software   §12.2
Sources of law   §1.1

Standing committees
    Assembly §6.5
    Senate §6.6
Stare decisis §5.1
State and federal law distinguished §1.4
State Bar of California
    Ethics §3.8
    In general §3.2
    Rules §3.3
    Sections §3.6
    See - Lawyers
State Board of Equalization §8.9
Statutes
    Numbering §6.7 et seq.
    Online sources §§12.5, 12.6
    Tips for finding §7.14
    See - Codes
    See - Legislation
Statutes at Large §6.10
Subsequent history table §5.12
Substance and procedure distinguished §1.4
Superior Court §§4.9, 5.9
Supplementation §2.11
Supreme Court
    California §4.7
    United States §4.5

Tables §2.4
Taxation law
    Practice resources §13.6
Terminology §1.16
Text books §9.4
Time deadlines in appellate process §5.11
Tips
    Finding administrative law §8.17
    Finding cases §5.16
    Finding current information §11.1
    Finding statutes §7.14
    General research tips §1.17
Tort law
    Practice resources §13.17
Transactions and litigation distinguished §1.4
Treatises
    In General §9.1
    Online sources §§12.5, 12.6
    Witkin §9.2

Trust law
     Practice resources   §13.7

Uniform laws
     California acts   §7.17
     In general   §7.16
Updating information   §11.1 et seq.
USCCAN   §6.18
United States Code   §7.4
United States Courts - see Federal courts
U.S. Code Congressional and Administrative
News   §6.18

Verifying authorities   §11.2

West
     CD-ROM   §§12.9, 12.10
     Digests   §5.20
     Key number system   §5.21
     Practice works   §10.9
     Reporter system   §5.15
     Software   §12.2
     Westlaw   §12.6
Witkin   §9.2
Workers' compensation law
     Practice resources   §13.13